Advance Praise

"Lorry Leigh Belhumeur has written a very personal, instructive and engaging book about childhood adversity and its consequences. Even better, she's put together a compelling and very useable approach to healing that incorporates not only her own amazing story, but those of others who have told her their stories."

—Jane Stevens, founder, publisher PACEs Connection
PACEsConnection.com,, ACEsTooHigh.com
PACEs = Positive and Adverse Childhood Experiences

"Wow, Lorry has a gripping story to tell and uplifting (though hard-won) advice to share. This book will change people's lives. The difficult truth is that many people have faced childhood traumas. For readers who may feel lost, unheard, unsupported, or alone, and have not had the tools to finally break intergenerational cycles, find peace, and experience gratitude and wellness, this book offers a lifeline."

—Beth Pickett, bestselling author of *College Admissions: The Essential Guide for Busy Parents*

"Mastering Resilience is one of the best books on a topic that has become a national necessity. Lorry Leigh Belhumeur is the real deal. A must read for anyone wanting to overcome adversity and create a bright future for themselves and the next generation."

—Sara Connell, founder of Thought Leader Academy and bestselling author of *The Science of Getting Rich for Women*

"Mastering Resilience is an incredible read for anyone willing to turn the pain of past trauma into a building block of a beautiful, purposeful life path. I have no doubt this gem will prove to be a valuable resource to many!"

—Alexandra Kuisis, bestselling author
of the award-winning memoir,
Truth Matters, Love Wins

"In this ground-bréaking, accessible book, mental health pioneer Lorry Leigh Belhumeur is a cycle breaker for the generations to come and will change untold lives affected by trauma. There is indeed a way to master resilience, and the process and mindset shifts are within these pages."

—Fabienne Fredrickson, author of
*Embrace Your Magnificence: Get Out of Your Own Way
and Live a Richer, Fuller, More Abundant Life,*
and founder of Fabienne.com and
the *Delicious Life* podcast.

MASTERING RESILIENCE

TRANSFORMING INTO YOUR PURPOSE

Lorry Leigh Belhumeur, Ph.D.

Printed in the United States of America

Hardcover ISBN: 978-1-958714-83-6
Paperback ISBN: 978-1-958714-84-3
Ebook ISBN: 978-1-958714-85-0
Library of Congress Control Number: 2023931950

CHICAGO·NEWYORK·PARIS·ROME

Muse Literary
3319 N. Cicero Avenue
Chicago IL 60641-9998

"If we help the children but don't meet the needs of the adults, our work will have little impact…You have to help the frontline adults who will be working with the children and youth."

—Bruce D. Perry, M.D., Ph.D. From the book, *What Happened to You? Conversations on Trauma, Resilience, and Healing* by Bruce D. Perry, M.D., Ph.D. and Oprah Winfrey

Mastering Resilience™ Resources

The Recipe for Mastering Resilience™

Before you dive into this book, I recommend that you download the free Recipe for Mastering Resilience™. This simple step by step process will act as a roadmap to help you get the desired results you are looking for in this book. I call it a recipe because there are specific ingredients, combined in a precise order, that will get you the outcome you want.

How far along are you on the Mastering Resilience Journey? Take this assessment to find out... In order to reach a new destination, we need to know our current location. In this quick assessment you'll find out where you are in relationship with each of the 8 mastering resilience ingredients. You'll learn your current score and after doing the exercises in the book, you can take the assessment again and celebrate your progress. Take the assessment now to start moving closer to your purpose immediately.

This 8-week transformational course teaches you step-by-step how to turn your past adversity into your purpose. Each week, a new ingredient is introduced, that provides specific content with guiding principles and mindset shifts that will take you through your journey of mastering resilience. You'll hear stories of real-life applications and be guided to integrate the content which will transform your thoughts, feelings and behaviors. Check out the course registration and details HERE:

 Super Resilient™ Youth
For those of you who are ready to get started right away with breaking the cycle in the next generation, there is the opportunity to positively impact the young people in your care. The Super Resilient™ Youth program, based on the recipe for mastering resilience, is a research-based mental wellness curriculum designed to empower youth to gain a deeper understanding of themselves to combat inner and external negativities in ways that build life-long resilience.

Disclaimer

Although the publisher and the author have made every effort to ensure that the information in this book was correct at press time and while this publication is designed to provide accurate information in regard to the subject matter covered, the publisher and the author assume no responsibility for errors, inaccuracies, omissions, or any other inconsistencies herein and hereby disclaim any liability to any party for any loss, damage, or disruption caused by errors or omissions, whether such errors or omissions result from negligence, accident, or any other cause.

This publication is meant as a source of valuable information for the reader; it is not meant as a substitute for direct expert assistance. If such a level of assistance is required, the services of a competent professional should be sought.

This book contains content that may be troubling to some readers, including, but not limited to, references to molestation, sexual assault, domestic violence, as well as verbal, physical, and emotional abuse.

Please be mindful of these and other possible triggers. If you find the content to be too difficult, please allow yourself to take a break and come back to reading when you are ready to continue your journey of Mastering Resilience. If you or a loved

one is contemplating hurting themselves, please call the National
Suicide Prevention Lifeline at 988.

I encourage you to practice self-care before, during, and after
reading. If you need support, please seek assistance if needed
from the resources on page 166.

Table of Contents

Prologue

*Owning our story and loving ourselves through that
process is the bravest thing that we'll ever do.*

—*Brené Brown*

I sat in the judge's chambers with my bangs curled, a turquoise barrette pinned in my light brown hair. As the judge walked in, we rose, and I smoothed out my white, knee-length eyelet dress. It was my only good outfit, and Mom had made me wear it for this occasion.

Without an ounce of sympathy in his voice, the judge glanced at his papers and asked me, "Do you want this man to be your dad?" He pointed in the direction of my stepfather—my mother's third husband—never making eye contact with me. My mind wandered, pondering the question as though it were new and not something I constantly debated.

"This man," my stepfather, had been a part of my life since I was five years old and now, at eleven, I knew his fondling was wrong. Only we weren't here to talk about any of that. I didn't want to get in trouble with my mom or the judge or any adult. It never occurred to me that this might've been the safest place to tell my truth.

Weeks prior, my mom had taken my brother and me on a road trip across the country to visit her first husband, the man whose name was on my birth certificate. When we finally arrived in the Midwestern city after hours and hours of driving, I was about to catapult out of the car. I desperately needed an ice cream cone, or headphones filled with loud music—anything to drown out my feelings. What was my mom doing? I hadn't seen her first husband since I was a toddler. Why did I need to meet him as a tween? And why did she insist I call him dad?

My brother and I watched from the backseat of the car. Mom rang the doorbell, waiting for the man I thought was my biological father to emerge. When he did, he was a tall, thin man with piercing eyes—my brother's eyes. He stepped out onto the porch and closed the door behind him. It was obvious; he didn't want Mom inside. Probably he didn't want us inside either. My brother and I exchanged looks. This wasn't going well. Not at all.

Mom turned around and waved her hand toward our direction as he glanced at the car and shook his head. We immediately got back in our seats. We knew the papers she brought with her were signed.

She started the car and began driving. A few minutes later, she casually said, "He didn't want to see you one last time." We knew the papers meant that he'd relinquished his parental rights. "He's no longer 'technically' your dad. I mean, it's no big deal, you guys didn't ever really know him."

But what if I wanted to know him? I thought about that road trip as my mind wandered back to the courtroom. *Do I want THIS man to be my dad?*

The more I thought about all this, the more it seemed like a trick question, not a matter of choice. My stepfather was already Dad. That's what I called him: Daddy, Dad, the only dad I knew.

This adoption was going to happen, whether I wanted it to or not, and I didn't want to upset Mom any more than I already did. I was trouble. Even though I did well in school, for her I was always too loud, too weepy, too angry, too emotional, or *not enough*.

I stood tall in my white, patent leather Mary Janes, staring coolly at the judge. "Yes, I do."

The adoption papers were finalized, and THIS man legally became my father. Throughout my life, I'd look back on this day, wondering, *What would have happened if I'd told the truth?*

*   *   *

Of course, the notion of one truth—*the truth*—especially applied to something as complicated as a human being is complicated.

Here's one truth, for more than three decades, I've been a licensed psychologist working in the field of children's mental health. The *Los Angeles & Times OC* recently named me a 2022 OC Visionary, a distinction fewer than sixty individuals receive. I'm a sought-after speaker and presenter on the topic of adverse childhood experiences (ACEs), resiliency, specializing in how mitigating the impact of the toxic stress response can impact the classroom and the future of our youth. I'm a mentor to psychologists, social workers, counselors, and psychologists, social workers, and counselors-in-training. I'm a wife. I'm a mother to two adult children. I'm a strong, resilient woman.

I'm also an adult with ACEs. Eight ACEs. And that number matters. As the ACE Resource Network explains, ACEs "cause our body's stress response systems to get stuck 'on' and disrupt our brains, our bodies, even our genes. These disruptions can affect us in childhood and have ripple effects throughout our lives." Eight ACEs.

This is my truth:

Abuse: physical, sexual, emotional.

Neglect: emotional (e.g., love withheld).

Family dysfunction: alcohol/substance misuse by a parent; parent with mental illness; parents' divorce; domestic violence.

Eight. And yet, that number only hints at a deeper story. A story where physical abuse meant spankings and spankings meant the Beetle Bopper—a small, hard, plastic baseball bat, part of a game called "Bop the Beetle." When the Beetle Bopper suddenly disappeared, my brother and I endlessly debated where it went. Decades later, he confessed he'd destroyed it so it couldn't be used as a weapon against us anymore.

A story where sexual abuse looked like silk pajamas for seven-year-old me, a present from one of my "dad's" deployments during the Vietnam War. A story where my mother believed I seduced her husband.

A story of learning to sleep with a pillow over my head to drown out my noise.

Of breaking into the medicine cabinet when I was ten and stealing Librium, an early anxiety medication, trying to numb the pain. Of cutting myself where clothes and shoes covered. Of trying to break my arm with a hammer.

Of being on the Honor Roll.

Five marriages, three divorces, one annulment, and one that left my mother a widow, five marriages, the first when I was an infant and the last when I was in college.

Of holidays glinting with rage. Massive fights.

Of "ripple effects," my first ulcer at age twenty-seven. Four miscarriages.

And there are adversities that I never experienced, nor will I. I'll never know discrimination because of the color of my skin. I'll never know what it's like to live with a parent who was incarcerated or addicted to drugs. I didn't know abject poverty or gunfire in the streets outside my house. It was the inside of my house that was unsafe, with multiple burglaries, the one most memorable was when a thief stole all the presents under the Christmas tree on Christmas Eve after my parents had placed them there.

Eight ACEs. And so many protective factors.

Teachers who believed in me. Access to a library and a Book Mobile. Faith. Sunday school, where I found solace and ritual and belief, where I had perfect attendance.

I had the opportunity to learn and practice responsibility and caring for others. Babysitting neighborhood children, earning my certification as a nurse's aide (CNA) and working in a skilled nursing facility in high school. I started working as a CNA at an inpatient psychiatric facility when I was twenty, the first year I spent Thanksgiving volunteering at the Venice Beach Soup Kitchen.

After my master's in Education, I taught undergraduate psychology while finishing my dissertation at UCLA. I also had a very successful private practice as an educational consultant, where I taught metacognitive strategies as study skills to elementary through high school students – leading them from D+ to A+ grades, resulting in higher self-esteem and confidence in themselves, my specialty. As I became a licensed psychologist, child and adolescence was my focus in private practice. I ultimately gravitated to community mental health and non-profit leadership, where my subject matter expertise in child trauma, and subsequent mastery of ACEs, with a focus on effective solutions to treat the impact of toxic stress caused by ACEs, was implemented in meaningful ways.

Eight ACES. And over 100,000 youth and families impacted by me and the ripple effect of the child psychologists, social workers, and counselors-in-training that I've supervised, teachers

I've trained, and the students I've taught, spanning more than three decades.

My truth—my truths—have led me to develop Mastering Resilience.™

*   *   *

I've always believed that something greater than me has shown me the good in the world. In the face of whatever adversity I've experienced, my faith in whom I choose to call God, and the hope of a better tomorrow has sustained me. It is that faith and hope that inspired me to develop the Mastering Resilience course.

According to students who've taken the course:

"This course is exactly what I needed."

"I experience life peace because of this course and these connections."

"My level of gratitude is through the roof."

"I hope you feel deep down how much I love and appreciate you and how much of a difference your class has made on me."

"I am closer to my life's goals than I've ever been, and I see them completed as a result of the learnings in this course."

Now, in this book, anyone who cares about breaking the cycle of trauma—psychologists, social workers, counselors, leaders of youth, teachers, parents, relatives, allies—can take action by applying the principles described in this book.

Too often, we are unable to provide what children need, because we haven't healed ourselves. The wounds of our ACEs still haunt and stifle us, impacting how we behave and how we feel and how we think. And when our mindset is negatively focused, and that's how we view the world, we're doing the exact opposite of breaking the cycle; we're perpetuating it.

Not all mental health conditions can be prevented. But some can. Just like diabetes. In some cases, it (diabetes) can't be prevented, and in other cases, we can see it coming. The risk factors are there, and with certain lifestyle changes, we can prevent the disease of diabetes from occurring. And in many cases, people with an unpreventable case of the disease of diabetes can receive proper treatment to live in wellness. Blood sugar can be regulated through a combination of interventions, including diet and medicine.

The same is true for mental health and wellness. Some conditions cannot be prevented and need proper medical, psychiatric, and effective psychological treatment, providing what is required to live in wellness. Of course, Mastering Resilience is not a substitute for mental health care. And because we understand and know certain circumstances that create the risk of depression and anxiety and post-traumatic stress disorder, we see them very clearly, and we can see them coming. The science is clear; without intervention, without buffering, without providing protective factors, mental unwellness will likely occur as a result of trauma, ACEs, and other adversities.

We have an obligation to do something about that; helping ourselves can be the first step. We don't have to wait until a child is in crisis to provide the very thing that they need to be supported and live in wellness and know their value.

This can also be our truth.

To the young people who have faced Adverse Childhood Experiences, including those who are now adults.

Description and meaning
of Kintsugi bowl.

K *intsugi*, meaning golden ("*kin*") and repair ("*tsugi*"), is a traditional Japanese art form where cracked pottery is repaired with liquid gold. Kintsugi is known worldwide as a symbol of healing from trauma. This bowl symbolizes that you are more valuable because adversity has strengthened you and your inner strength is a beautiful thing.

Introduction

In high school, I used to bake cakes from scratch. Though the cake mix packages at the grocery store were tantalizing, I preferred my own recipe. I would break each egg individually; the extra-large white ones, which are still my favorite, would sometimes have two yolks. I'd stir them in a glass bowl, where I could watch the yolks and whites conjoin. Melted butter and milk moistened the eggs, yielding an even brighter yellow. Then there was the magic of adding sugar and spices, changing the batter's consistency in the glass bowl, a smooth mixture, almost oven ready. Ultimately, sifting in the flour thickened the batter, and once the oven reached the desired temperature, the cake was ready to be baked.

The process of making a cake is easy—you follow a recipe with a set of ingredients and instructions.

In life, however, when handling adversities and beginning or continuing along your healing journey, there are no specific instructions—especially as we break intergenerational cycles. That's why I created the recipe for Mastering Resilience, which is a simple step-by-step process for transforming into your purpose. It's simple, though not necessarily easy. And just like baking a cake, you get to learn to be well versed in techniques and ingredients. Bakers know all their ingredients ahead of time. They know each ingredient's specific qualities and characteristics and how those qualities and characteristics work together to make a delicious cake. The ingredients are added in a particular order, and the cake is baked in the right conditions. It doesn't work if you put some of the ingredients in the bowl, pour them into a pan, bake it, and then pull it out of the oven and crack an egg on top. Talk about disaster!

The egg is added at just the right time, to aerate the batter, for the protein of the egg to break down and recombine with other ingredients to give the cake body and structure (and deliciousness). Likewise, the recipe for mastering resilience involves identifying the necessary ingredients and learning how to combine them. And key mindset shifts (or baking conditions) will help you to get the outcome you desire for your life, time after time.

*   *   *

Many years ago, I attended Fabienne Fredrickson's three-day workshop The Mindset Retreat™. It was there that I learned once and for all how to shift my thinking—and what powerful results that small action could have. She taught that you could change your entire trajectory just by the way you thought about something. When you decide, "I have a choice to think differently," the most fundamental aspects of your existence—experiences, identity, likes, and dislikes—become adjustable.

Though mindset shifts weren't a new concept, they were new to me at the time, and these shifting thoughts can make or break what we're trying to accomplish in our lives. According to psychologist Carol Dweck, whose theories of intelligence are some of the most influential today, there are two main mindsets: growth mindset and fixed mindset. In a growth mindset, you believe in yourself enough to shift mental blocks that may be preventing you from achieving your ultimate goals. A growth mindset allows you to challenge yourself while focusing on your future and celebrating each milestone along the way. When you have a fixed mindset, you firmly believe that you cannot change. You are the way you are, and you are either inherently good at something, or inherently bad at something.

If you want to learn how to play tennis and you have a fixed mindset, you might say to yourself, 'I've never been good at sports, so why should I even try?' If you have a growth mindset, you may say, 'while I haven't been particularly good at sports in the past, maybe it would be fun to try a new activity. Maybe I'll be good at it one day!' The process of mastering resilience requires a growth mindset rather than a fixed one.

Throughout this book, you'll experience mindset shifts about what you're capable of accomplishing along this healing journey. You'll have the opportunity to identify the stories you tell yourself, the stories you tell yourself about yourself, the stories you tell yourself about the adversity you faced, the stories you tell yourself about the future, etc. Most importantly, you'll learn to create mindset shifts that are growth minded, positively focused, and effective in shifting your perspective forward rather than further into the past.

Reliving adversities you experienced won't necessarily help you move forward in a positive way. When you get in touch with your intrinsic value (i.e., when you KNOW you have value), you behave differently toward yourself and the world around you. Even though you may have experienced childhood trauma or faced major adversity in your life in the past, I want you to know that you're not alone, and that there is hope. Hope can come in many forms.

You'll learn that you have the ability--and the capacity--to create a future based on loving yourself and showcasing your intrinsic value to the outside world. Of course, loving yourself may not happen overnight. That's why we'll practice exercises to help you seek truth and clarity about yourself and your worth. As you navigate your past and your future, you'll discover strategies that will allow you to master your own resilience, once and for all. We'll cover the proven process of taking control of your inner dialog and begin shifting these thoughts, so you hear undeniable self-love. When you encounter negative self-talk, you'll have tools to positively shift your perspective. You'll become crystal clear about your intentions on this healing journey and learn to identify your own unique qualities. By reading this book, you'll begin to truly understand the connection between thoughts, feelings, actions, and belief patterns, and how these can affect your perception of your value. While you're mastering resilience, we'll also cover ways to give grace, forgive, understand, and become compassionate toward others who have made mistakes or harmed you, causing you to feel less than your undeniable worth. You'll embrace your intrinsic value.

Mindset Shift: I am capable of breaking the cycle in this generation.

And yet, if you're like me, your own adversities have not stopped you from caring for others. Loving others. Mentoring others. If you're like me, you've felt called to help each new generation do it better. At times, you've been studious when you should have been reckless, reckless when you should have been studious, and you've forgiven yourself for those mistakes. As my peers, other leaders, influencers and allies of youth, it's critical that we understand what it takes to work through our own emotions and wounds to continue the journey of healing ourselves, to be present, intentional in our actions, and to give others the freedom to do the same. You know there's something inside of your soul that urges you to do whatever it takes to heal. You know when you do, you'll be more impactful.

I want to give my peers tools to master their own resilience so they can break the cycle once and for all. My own healing journey and life experiences have prepared me to guide you on this journey to knowing your intrinsic value, getting unstuck, finding your purpose, and realizing that you, too, can become a master of resilience in your own life, to live on purpose in order to help others do the same. In this book, I've consolidated my decades of clinical experience as a psychologist, supervisor, mentor, teacher, and leader--as well as my own healing journey--to help you master the recipe for mastering resilience so you can help others do the same.

Many years ago, I saw a TEDMED talk by pediatrician, Dr. Nadine Burke Harris, who later became the first Surgeon General of the State of California. In her talk, she explained the Adverse Childhood Experiences (ACE) research that makes the connection between childhood trauma and physical and mental health challenges later in life.

This was a call to action to confront the prevention and treatment of trauma head-on, and I took that call to action seriously. I poured over the science of ACEs, including the original CDC-Kaiser Permanente Adverse Childhood Experiences Study, or ACE Study, conducted by Drs. Vincent Felitti and Robert Anda, and others, that kickstarted ACEs research. I was trained by Dr. Anda to teach others about the study as well as the neuroscience that explains how "what happened to you" gets embedded in the brain and body. I discovered from Dr. Bruce D. Perry, co-author of the book, *What Happened to You*, that "(this) phrase originated (decades ago) in the pioneering work group of

Dr. Sandra Bloom, developer of the Sanctuary Model." I learned during my earlier exposure to the ACE science to ask this question in my clinical practice, as well as "what's strong with you." These are phrases intended to replace the question, "what's wrong with you?" that was frequently spoken in the past to address children's "unpleasant" behavior that bothered the adults in their lives.

I also learned how **hope can come from understanding neuroplasticity** (our brains' ability to rewire), and why discovering the types of help that best assist those who experienced trauma is so crucial.

As I trained audiences of teachers, teachers-in-training, psychologists, counselors, counselors-in-training, court-appointed special advocates (CASA workers), and other leaders and influencers of youth, I started to notice something. Those teachers, psychologists, counselors, CASA workers, and leaders who'd dedicated their lives to serving youth had levels of childhood adversity that mirrored the level of ACEs of children and youth with mental health disorders that were or had been in my care. It became clear to me that **the children who had high levels of childhood trauma often will become adults in positions that influence and heal the next generation.**

I took a retrospective view of my personal and professional life and reverse engineered what worked and what didn't. I created my own framework—a winning recipe, if you will—to ensure that you, too, can master resilience and get unstuck, by turning your past adversities into the fuel that motivates you to live your life on purpose for your impact on the world. The recipe for mastering resilience is a strategy to use on your healing journey

With my recipe, you will break cycles, cause a ripple effect, and shift the trajectory of the next generation. Together, we have an opportunity to positively impact today's youth in ways that will help them be more confident, experience their innate value and self-worth, and live a life of purpose. We can significantly reduce the instances of physical and mental health disorders in today's children.

Whether you're a pediatrician, child psychologist or counselor, a coach, a nurse, or a teacher, there's a good chance that you, like me, gravitated toward a helping profession because you've experienced adversity of many kinds. Perhaps you're a parent, or other caregiver, committed to the children in your care. You are here for a reason. You have father injuries, mother injuries, childhood adversities in one form or another.

You're successful in your own right, but your gut knows that you could do more to break the cycle of abuse, neglect, and family dysfunction for the next generation. You set out on your own healing journey, either independently or with help, yet you still get triggered and behave in ways that aren't congruent with the best version of yourself. You have dozens of self-help books on your nightstand, the coffee table, the bookcase--"shelf-help books," they're often referred to, because, for various reasons, they can be hard to take off the proverbial shelf and apply them to your life. Maybe the self-help strategies you used don't work anymore, or maybe it seems you've tried every available option. Maybe you've experienced traditional forms of therapy, and those designed specifically to address trauma such as Trauma-Focused Cognitive-Behavioral Therapy (TF-CBT), Eye Movement Desensitization and Reprocessing (EMDR), or other modalities like Neuro-Linguistic Programming (NLP), meditation, hypnotherapy, and others. Maybe they've helped to alleviate that incongruous stress response you so often experience. Yet you know you have more healing to do on your life's journey.

You have so much love in your heart that was created and refined through adversity, and still, you feel stuck. You want to heal more deeply. You want to be confident that you're breaking the cycle in this generation. And deep down, you know that you can only influence the youth, whether your own children, your students, patients, clients, the team you coach, or others in your care, to the extent that you've done your own healing work. You desperately want to help the next generation, and you also know that your impact on the world will be even greater when you get unstuck and start living your life as the highest version of yourself, with purpose.

To pay it forward, to help children master resilience from their adversity, you get to first understand and apply the method to yourself. The best, most resilient version of you will be well-prepared to teach the future generation what you have learned-- and equip them to do the same.

Maybe you picked up this book because you're ready to live a full and authentic life while being in the present moment rather than stuck in the past. Maybe you picked up this book because you're ready to live abundantly, replacing negative self-talk with positive affirmations and aspirational goals. Or, maybe you picked up this book because you're a leader who works with children and youth, and/or you're a parent and you feel a greater sense of urgency to heal once and for all for the sake of your children. You're ready to change the way children perceive adversity, and you want them to become stronger at a young age. You want them to know and understand the possibilities that they, too, can become stronger from past experiences and can bounce back from any mistake. You have boots on the ground and you know that you cannot wait for funding or policy decisions to trickle down in the future to help children. Yes, they will help eventually, and you also know you must act now. You want a proven solution.

If you're ready to make this commitment, demonstrate what self-love looks like for future generations, and master resilience so you can become more comfortable with your own intrinsic value, keep reading. You will feel deserving and worthy of all the abundance that life has to offer you by the time you finish this book. I'm proud of you for reading this far, and I'm excited to go on this incredible healing journey with you. You are here to make a commitment to BE the role model of an authentic, loving, and powerful being and to demonstrate what self-love looks like to future generations, as a master of resilience, so they can also choose to be confident and comfortable in their own skin. It starts with you.

Whether you're twenty, thirty, sixty, or seventy years old, this is the perfect time--and the right time--to heal from past adversity for your own sake and for the sake of the children. It's entirely possible to interact with a child with confidence, knowing your worth and your own intrinsic value so they can do the same. According to the *Stanford Encyclopedia of Philosophy*, "The intrinsic value of something is said to be the value that that thing has 'in itself,' or 'for its own sake,' or 'as such,' or 'in its own right.'" Intrinsic value can also be defined as inherent worth. Value is inherent in your very existence. Everyone on this planet has value because they exist.

My definition of intrinsic value is the experience that you have when you know you have value, regardless of what anyone around you says about you. It's the ability to go inward and feel love and acceptance for yourself because you know your true self, your compassionate self, your loving self, your authentic self-- whoever that is, regardless of what is going on around you or what anyone else says. Maybe you believe you are a child of God, maybe you believe you're ONE with the universe, or maybe you allow yourself to just BE without having to do anything-- and in that space, you feel your value.

It is my hope that by reading this book, you will feel loved, wanted, deserving, and worthy of all the abundance and joy that life has in store for you.

I'm so grateful to take you along this journey with me.

CHAPTER ONE

Creating the Optimal Conditions for Mastering resilience: Your Big Why

New research from the CDC found that, during the COVID-19 pandemic, suicide attempts among adolescents with four or more ACEs was twenty-five times as high as among adolescents without ACEs (Anderson et al., 2022). Now is the time to heal so you can break the cycle and step up to fight the youth mental health crisis.

*   *   *

Even though my "dad" introduced me to adult sexuality at the age of seven, I was still able to have a relationship with him as an adult, after he and my mom divorced. Surprisingly, in the face of domestic chaos, he was the stable one, the predictable one, the one who believed in me and told me I could be successful at anything I put my mind to. He was the one who seemed to counteract the impact of my mom's intermittent rage toward me. The one, who, in retrospect, created a warped sense of paternal dependence, a distorted view of love, and laid the foundation for experiencing a classic case of Stockholm syndrome well into adulthood.

As an adult, it was common for my "dad" and me to grab a bite, a quick breakfast, a casual dinner. One evening when I was in my early twenties, he and I were having dinner at a steakhouse. We were having drinks and making small talk instead of browsing the menu, when, jokingly, I said, "How come I don't look like anybody in the family?"

My mom was naturally thin. Many called her skinny, which she hated. My brother, at 6'2", was also extremely slender. Both had dark brown eyes. "You're just a big girl," Mom and Dad would say when I compared myself to them. My hazel eyes held a hint of the truth.

He took a gulp of his beer and set it down on the table, without looking at me.

"Ask your mom."

"Oh, c'mon, I was kidding."

"Lorry, it's not my place to tell you."

I left the restaurant before taking the first sip of my own drink and drove to my mom's house. Though I usually listened to rock music in the car in those days, I drove in silence, thinking about what I was going to say when I saw my mother.

Hey, Mom, who is my real dad?

Hey, Mom, was I unwanted?

Hey, Mom, why do all my father figures abandon me? Is it because of you?

When I got to her house, I knocked loudly on the dusty, gray aluminum door; the doorbell rarely worked. I heard her flip flops slapping. When the door opened, she greeted me with a half-smile. I could never tell if it was a genuine smile, a passive- aggressive smile, or another sort of smile. Smiles can be deceiving.

"I know why you're here," she said matter-of-fact. "Your dad called." I found out later that he'd rushed home to call her before I got there.

"Can I come in?"

She opened the door and turned away.

I walked into my childhood home, where pictures hung down the entire length of the hallway, and meaningless knickknacks cluttered the living room. I looked around, thankful that I could provide for myself. Once I'd left for university, I vowed I'd never live in the same house as my mother again.

She walked down the hall to her bedroom. In retrospect, that's where we had our most poignant conversations in my childhood. She paced around the room. I stood in the doorway.

"I considered telling you I was raped," she said, swiftly, emotionless. "Then I wouldn't have to tell you the truth."

"What's the truth, Mom?"

She stopped mid-step, and just for a second, I saw her face go stone-cold.

"You know all those cards you got on your birthdays and graduations from the older woman I told you was your babysitter? Well, that's your grandmother."

I felt the color leave my face.

She reached for her glass of wine on the rocks. "You want one? You might like to have one."

"No thank you, I'm okay."

"So, you know, I got divorced when you were just six months old," explained my mom, "but your brother's father (she said his name) wasn't your father."

My mind flew to that car ride to the Midwest. I stopped and stared at her and went deeper in thought.

So, wait, my brother and I are half-siblings? We don't have the same dad? I won't be able to donate a kidney to him if he needs one. What a weird thought...

"I had an affair. You were conceived in love. He was the love of my life. Your biological father said he would wait for me to get divorced. But he enlisted in the military, left town, and married someone else."

Wait. What? Who all knows? My real paternal grandparents, my "dad," clearly my biological father--who else? How can they all know and not me!?!?!

Somehow, I remained upright, processing this information. I'd spent twenty-two years thinking I knew my family. Apparently, I had no idea. I thought I knew all the secrets of the family.

Enraged, frustrated, confused, and sad--I felt the emotions boil up as my mom relayed this new information to me. Later, I would learn the whole story from my biological father—that he did wait, but my mom refused to leave her husband for many months; that he'd left in despair.

My identity coalesced around paternal abandonment. All three of these father figures renounced their role in some way. Could my shame go deeper? It did. I felt ashamed that the first dad (who I believed was my biological father for so long but was actually my brother's and not mine) wrote me off. I felt ashamed that I still received love from my adoptive dad while I was also obligated to have a relationship with him (that is, if I wanted to feel even remotely supported by a parent). And, of course, I felt ashamed that the person who had "become" my biological father knew all about me, all along, and seemingly wanted out.

My "daddy" wounds were not the only reason I was driven to become a psychologist and help others heal.

*   *   *

Years later, an intern named Alex sat in my well-lit, bright white office. He wore crimson pants, and there was a stain on his wrinkled, yellow button-up shirt. His dark brown hair was tangled—he had walked in mentioning his desperate need of a haircut. "No time for that," he said.

He pulled out his files and slowly handed them over to me.

"Lorry, I just don't know what to do here." His hand stroked his non-existent beard. "The parents are getting a divorce, and their seven-year-old and nine-year-old girls are distraught."

I looked at him solemnly, pushing my own emotions aside. A good therapist listens with a third ear, beyond words. We empathize without sympathizing.

"The dad is refusing visits and child support for the seven-year-old." Alex sighed heavily, as he always did when relaying this sort of information to me. "Do we tell her that the reason her dad doesn't want to see her is because she's not his biological daughter?"

My skin prickled, and I drew in a quick breath. My mind flashed back to a time when I, too, thought I knew who my biological father was. I hadn't known the truth until after my twenty-second birthday.

The room came back into present as Alex asked, "Lorry? What do you think? Can you help me with this case?"

I stared at him without an ounce of emotion.

"No, Alex, this one's too close to home. We'll find someone else who can help you."

As Alex left my office, I began to recognize why I couldn't supervise that case. Thoughts of my younger self--my younger *shame*--clouded my mind; I knew those thoughts would ultimately cloud my judgment. Wasn't it the mom's responsibility to tell her daughter who her father was? My anger simmered, and I felt hot tears spring to my eyes as I thought about my own childhood, and the hundreds of children I'd helped throughout my ten years as a psychologist and supervisor up to that point. Although I'd been in therapy myself for many years, I had a stark realization; I still had more healing to do to create a positive, bright future not only for myself, but for those I wanted to help. I wanted to break the cycle of having a victim mentality, yet I knew that if I continued to be triggered and rendered ineffective, I would have a harder time living out my purpose to help others heal. I needed to work even deeper on myself to make these dreams a reality.

*   *   *

The first ingredient of recipe for mastering resilience is creating the optimal conditions for mastering resilience: your BIG Why. It's critically important to have a destination in mind when beginning a journey. You're on a journey of healing, growing, and mastering resilience to transform into your purpose. To do so, you get to establish your "BIG Why."

Many of you may say that your BIG Why includes breaking a cycle to help the next generation, and to be sure, that was part of mine. Your BIG Why inspires you. It's your reason for being; the reason you choose to heal. Some say it's their "calling," their purpose in life. It's the main reason you help others and are resolute in your decision to become a master of resilience. It's tied to the impact you want to have in the world as you choose to live with purpose. It's the desired life you want to create for yourself. Consider it the legacy you want to leave. Regardless, **your BIG Why is the future you create when success is the only option**.

Your BIG Why often develops over time. If you don't know it yet, that's understandable and it's okay. All lives have purpose. Sometimes the very things that have hurt us, the adversity we've faced, and our journey are the very things that will give people hope and a purpose. It gives meaning to our mourning, our sadness, our circumstances––and to the adversity we faced.

*   *   *

When was the last time you considered your purpose in the world? The process of fully understanding your reason for being starts with reflecting on your overall purpose, and what inspires you toward the vision you have for your life in the future and/ or your legacy––your BIG Why. You don't have to know exactly what it is. For now, you can borrow mine, if you want to. Many people I know (and have the honor of working with) have a purpose statement included in their description of their BIG Why like mine that includes this statement.

My purpose is to be a cycle breaker for the next generation.

Throughout the various lectures and talks I've given, therapists, teachers, social workers, counselors, parents, and CASA workers have shared similar stories. They know they are here to break the cycle for the next generation. They've learned so much about themselves and the impact that their thoughts, feelings, and behaviors have on themselves and those around them. Yet, they're just not sure how to take the next steps.

We're going to spend some quality time on the topic of your BIG Why. It's time to give yourself the gift of being crystal clear on your BIG Why. You may have heard this concept defined as your reason for being. Authors and motivational speakers, among others, say you must know your BIG Why to determine your target, your true North, before beginning any journey. Some of you may have determined that your BIG Why is breaking a cycle to help the next generation. For others, stating or identifying their reason for being isn't so simple. Perhaps it's the possibility of a life no longer controlled or rendered helpless by the past. A life where you own your own choices and decisions, knowing exactly what you want and who you get to BE in the process. A life imagining exactly what it will look like when the cycle is broken.

Mindset Shift: To help others, I get to help myself first.

Let's start the process of identifying, defining, and/or refining your BIG Why.

Identify: Whether it's meditation, walking, listening to music, or something else entirely, go to a quiet place in your mind's eye. Start by identifying and/or defining the qualities and characteristics of who you are now, those qualities that you want to continue to tap into, and the qualities and characteristics of the person you would like to become—the person you get to be in this lifetime. Ask yourself what impact you truly want to make in the world. Identify the impact in detail to initiate your elaborate, decadent outcome of your healing journey. If you find yourself struggling at any point, come back to this step. I encourage you to spend the time you need. Documenting your purpose and your BIG Why in detail functions as a guide for your journey and the roadmap to help you get back on track. This is your vision of the life that you want for yourself and the impact you see yourself having. It will allow you to understand and learn more about yourself than you previously thought you did.

First, remind yourself of the YOU that you want to become-- the best qualities and characteristics of the person you'd like to become. Then identify your future state; see yourself at a specific location, time, and place.

In job interviews, we're often asked to think about where we see ourselves in five years. You may've once said, "I see myself taking the lead on implementing our company's strategic goals, since I enjoy taking leadership roles as seen in my previous work." A teacher taking my Mastering Resilience course said, "I'd love to be working at this incredible school, collaborating with other teachers and staff, as well as trying out new tools, ideas, and educational resources with the students in order to provide them with fantastic opportunities later in life." Alex, my former intern, once admitted, "I want the next generation to understand they have a loving adult who cares about them, and I want to be that loving adult to them."

Grab a sheet of paper and your favorite pen. Sit in a quiet place—a place where you can properly reflect on your past, your present, and your future.

The following questions come from my Mastering Resilience course. Answer them in detail while you're in a reflective state of mind. Think about your future:

Who do you share your life with?

What kinds of people do you get to be surrounded by? Are they leaders or emerging leaders? Peers? Positive people? "Successful" people?

What are your relationships like?

What are your friends like?

What are your feelings toward them?

What are you doing that you love most in your life?

What do you do socially?

What are you doing that is so much fun?

Do you want or have financial freedom? What does that look like?

Where do you work? What IS your work?

What's your income?

What kind of possessions do you have?

What is your lifestyle?

How are you contributing? What does that look like?

Where do you see yourself living? Is it in the same city you're currently living in? Your answer may surprise you.

What does your future home look and feel like?

What qualities and characteristics of YOU get to shine in this future state?

What does it feel like to be successful and happy in your own life?

What does "Living on Purpose, for a Purpose" mean to you?

Imagine: Allow yourself to imagine and visualize all of it. Feel the emotions borne of imagining this life, as if it already exists. Imagine the feeling that results from knowing the impact that you are having because you know your true purpose and you are living it out. Feel the smile come across your face, feel thriving. You get to sleep well, be happy, and be healthy. You get to enjoy your life. The past no longer affects your perception of your capabilities in this new version of yourself. Take a breath and imagine how much that fills you.

Mindset Shift: My past no longer reflects the new version of myself.

If you become overwhelmed at any point, go back to identifying your future state. During this process, it's also important to remember that the journey to healing takes time, energy, and effort, and failing is never an option. Going backwards to your past and how you were before you opened this book no longer serves your best and highest good. In this version of you, it is no longer an option to ruminate over the past because you love yourself and care about your vision for your future that much. There's no room for failure because you're growing and becoming the best version of yourself every single day. You now have the unique opportunity to paint this new, beautiful, gorgeous picture for yourself and what it looks like to be fully living out your purpose making the impact that you want to make in the world. Parts of you may be resistant right now due to whatever you've experienced in the past. You get to replace this resistance with resilience. Consider what steps you took to overcome obstacles in the past (so you can reassure yourself that you can do it) and think about how you'll become more resilient while advocating for yourself and creating the future you truly deserve.

Strategize: After you write down your answers to the questions in Identify, open a new sheet of paper in this same state of mind. Flip the paper so it's horizontal. Draw a big circle on the left-hand side of the sheet. Label this circle as "Point A." On the right-hand side of the piece of paper, draw another big circle, and label this one "Point B." Now draw a line connecting Point A and Point B. This is the line encompassing your overall strategy for your healing journey (hint: ultimately, it will not be a straight line). This line represents your roadmap to resilience, to solidifying your next-level vision of your future self. Empower yourself by participating in this activity.

Point A

Your **Point A** is the point of perception, decision or recognition that **you have a purpose**, in the context of past circumstances. Your Point A is the place of recognition of where you are relative to your past; where you are now is where you came from, which means it's also how far you've come. You're here for a reason. To begin any journey, it's critical to understand your starting point, including the connection between what occurred in the past, what you've overcome up to this point, and who you are in this moment. You've come a long way.

Early in my career, before I had children, I attended a women's retreat designed for women to get in touch with their spirituality and purpose in life. When I attended this retreat, I realized the importance of fully comprehending my starting place. I was able to identify my Point A, within the context of the adversity I'd faced as a child and of the ensuing destructive self-image that I carried with me. My Point A included the realization that I am who I am partly because I had the mother I had.

From there, I could imagine and strategize my end goals; I knew I wanted to help people. From an early age, I knew I would be in a helping profession. At the time, I thought it meant I would be a nurse or a teacher. Though the trajectory changed, the end goal was the same. The strategy I learned at this retreat greatly influenced me throughout my healing journey. I started with what I identified as my Point A, and acknowledged the progress that I made up to that point as I set out to move toward my Point B – that is to come.

I reverse-engineered what worked in my life. I eventually shifted the question of "what's wrong with me?" to "what happened to me? And then furthermore, "what's strong with me? What worked? What is the evidence of resilience that I've already demonstrated? Of all the experiences in my life, connecting my progress toward my end goals and back to my own starting point, has been one of the most pivotal points in my life. In other words, I measured my own progress from my starting point and not to anyone else's current situation. I acknowledged my own progress, how far I'd come, and that was so affirming.

Alex established his Point A as well. When the process of undertaking a healing journey came up in supervision, Alex said to me, "Lorry, I think my Point A, who I am at this current time, is the product of the years as a young child who witnessed abuse in my house growing up.. But I thought it was normal at the time...yet, I internalized what I saw and I believed that I wasn't worthy and that I wasn't good enough to help others. Since working with you, though, and seeing all these cases come through, I now have a better understanding of how I help others...the strengths that I've already demonstrated along the way. Yet, I also understand that to help others, I must help myself. That's where I'm starting from."

Part of identifying your Point A is also to understand that **sometimes the very adversity we face is what inspires us and fuels our purpose.** In Alex's case at this point, it fueled his desire to help others.

Other aspects of our Point A are the parts of us that have not yet healed. For example, adversity often results in the development of an inner critic. The inner critic may show up as haunting thoughts about our past. They may tell us what we're unable to accomplish because of past experiences. They may even discourage us from becoming our best selves. We're so hard on ourselves. That inner critic may always, in some respect, be there. However, it *is* possible to get to the point where your inner critic doesn't control your thoughts and your future experiences. One of the best ways to handle your inner critic is to simply expect it, add it to your Point A and honor it for the purpose it served in the past, love it, and you will be able to let it go through this mastering resilience journey.

Mindset Shift: My inner critic served a purpose in the past, and I control my future.

Point B

Your **Point B** is the future self you described earlier. It's your BIG Why.

Point B is your next-level self. It's your future vision of the best version of yourself—the best version you can ultimately be in your lifetime. The healing journey we'll take through this book will ultimately lead you toward your Point B, where you have transformed the adversities in your past into something that is meaningful and purposeful.

Let's go back to your notes when you imagined your future self. These notes apply to your Point B. In fact, the answers you provided to these questions encompass Point B.

When Alex began this exercise, he envisioned himself helping others. But he soon realized that to help others, he knew it was important for him to help himself be the best version of himself. To do so, he visualized his future. He discovered that he'd like to run with his husky, Rusty, every morning before work. He wanted to be able to take his future family on a beautiful, luxurious vacation at least once a year. He envisioned renting a beach house for an upcoming family reunion with his aunts, uncles, cousins, and extended family.

Alex acknowledged his Point A, and he recognized that his ultimate healing journey would lead him to embody his Point B— the life he'd always dreamed of for himself and for his family. He also acknowledged the progress he'd made on his healing journey already. He reverse-engineered what had already worked for him and decided to do more of what worked––and less of what didn't.

"Lorry, but how will I be able to dedicate the time and energy to go on this healing journey? What if I fail? What if…"

I looked at him with a knowing smile. He stopped himself from going down the rabbit hole of negative thinking.

"The journey will be on your own schedule, Alex. That line you drew connecting the two circles isn't only a line. It's also a series of squiggles and puzzle pieces. A fantastical journey you get to create for yourself," I told him. "Sure, there's work to be done. To experience the joy during the journey of healing, you recognized Point A as the most critical part of your overall healing journey. Since you're already able to acknowledge this for yourself, you won't fail. And, if you define something as a failure, you can always reframe it and ask yourself, what if this circumstance is actually happening for me and not against me?"

Alex nodded, connecting the dots for himself.

Mindset Shift: I can and I will navigate my life toward my BIG Why.

I repeated myself to Alex, "the work is simple, but it may not always be easy, and you may find yourself in a slump from time to time. That's normal. Once you embark on this healing path, though, you'll find so much happiness and true joy on the journey toward your Point B."

Like Alex, I want you, too, to acknowledge that this work may be simple––not necessarily easy. Reading this book in and of itself does not create the transformation. How often have we purchased books, read at least a portion of them, and not applied anything we've read. Doing the exercises, taking mental breaks, and allowing yourself to be inspired by your Point B and completing the work necessary will prove your commitment to yourself and to your own healing journey. Your BIG Why will be your inspiration. It's no longer a daydream. It's no longer a "What If?" statement in your vocabulary. Your BIG Why is achievable. If you choose not to take the steps to blend these ingredients together, you may still be on autopilot a year from now, or ten years from now, and nothing will change for you. If you take these steps, blending and mixing the ingredients of this recipe, you'll be closer to mastering resilience, healing, and becoming your best self. When you follow the recipe, you'll create the future life you want for yourself.

*   *   *

Diane was a life coach I hired earlier in my career. I had a thriving private practice and was a sought-after supervisor. I was considered successful. My clients saw amazing positive results, and my supervisees (including Alex) experienced professional growth and development. But something was off.

I consulted with Diane, a coach from Klemmer, "a premiere resource for leadership and character development" as referenced on their website, Klemmer.com. I was expecting simple answers as to why negative thoughts (my inner critic) continued stirring around my head. I was great at helping others with their own negative thoughts, right? Why couldn't I handle my own?

Diane gave me an assignment. The first part of this assignment was to write down a list of the negative things I told myself--the things the inner critic said. Then, she said, put on an uplifting song--a positive song, a powerful song--and let the words of the song sink in while tearing up the piece of paper with all the negative comments I'd just written down. Let the words of the song sink in. Then, take the pieces of paper and burn them (in a safe place).

It was a good assignment. Experience the feeling, the confidence, and the joy that comes with the uplifting music. The empowering music makes you feel invincible, and at the same time, destroys the negative words. Got it. Except I didn't get it; I didn't complete it. I woke up in the morning and remembered

I hadn't finished the assignment. I hadn't taken the final step to burn the words.

Before I left for work, I ripped up the paper into tiny pieces, put them in a mason jar, threw some stick matches into the jar, and put the jar in the cup holder of my car. I drove to the end of the street, found a good place to park--a safe place to burn pieces of paper filled with negative comments. I got out of the car and squatted down in some bushes, definitely not the intent of the assignment, and proceeded to attempt to burn the strips of paper. The day was windy. The papers singed, but nothing burned to ashes. I was late for work. School buses packed with children turned down the street. I had to look suspicious, squatting in the bushes. So, with my handwritten words still visible on the papers, I put the burned stick matches in the jar, screwed the lid on tight, and threw the jar on the floor of the back seat of my car.

Every time I drove that week, I was reminded of those tiny, charred scraps of paper with the negative things. And my incomplete assignment. I heard the *clinkety, clinkety, clink* every time I turned a corner, as the stick matches hit the jar, rolling around from side to side on the floor of my back seat.

The following week, during my coaching session with Diane, I admitted that I hadn't finished the assignment. I told her the jar was still on the dark gray floorboard of my car.

"Go to your car right now and get that jar," Diane insisted.

I did as I was told. I unlocked my white Toyota Camry, picked up the mason jar, and tucked it safely in my armpit.

"Get it as far away from your body as you can," Diane declared, as if she could see me.

There I was on the sidewalk with my arm extended as far as it would go, holding the jar with all the negative comments I told myself daily: "I'm fat, I'm broken, I'm unlovable, I'm a piece of ..."

The negative thoughts were singed, but still visible in the glass jar with the lid screwed tight.

"Take it to a trash can."

"But there's someone sitting on the bench next to the trash can," I said, heading in the opposite direction.

"You're having a hard time letting go, aren't you? It'll be okay if you throw it in the trash can where you can't retrieve it."

I know what it's like to want to, to need to, to hang on to hateful words like a warm, snuggly security blanket. To let go might feel like abandoning our own identity. And, somehow, holding onto imposter syndrome felt like protection. But holding onto it no longer served me. Diane's words of encouragement and permission were all I needed. I turned around and marched to the trash can. Carefully, intentionally, I set down the mason jar. All the hateful, self-loathing comments, all the way at the bottom, never to be seen again.

*   *   *

The next morning, I got a call. "Can I come see you, Dr. Lorry?"

I immediately headed to my office. My client, Nancy, entered my doorway promptly at 9:00 a.m. She sulked onto the black leather couch and hugged her knees to her chest. She started sobbing. Our discussions occasionally produced tears, but nothing to this level. I've had sessions where clients cry for forty-five minutes without saying a word, so I knew that she needed me to wait until she was ready to speak.

She garnered the courage to speak. "I want...to...die." Nancy said, in between fits of tears, "I'm a piece of shit."

"I'm a piece of shit" was a phrase I often heard from clients in my office and from those with an inaccurate self-image who felt bad about themselves. On this particular day, I froze in place. My mouth became dry, and I felt a single tear drop behind my glasses.

Sometimes the breakthrough is instantaneous. One of the slips of paper in the jar I had just thrown away the day before had those exact words written on it. A shiver ran down my spine. I realized in that moment that by my letting go of my own belief of being "a piece of shit," Nancy would be able to do the same. She was able to receive the care she needed to get through her crisis. When I saw her in a future session, she acknowledged that the words that she told herself about herself had led to her mental health crisis.

Mindset Shift: My own healing is directly related to freeing others to do the same.

Breaking the cycle can be as easy as identifying "what it is." What is the cycle and what appears to perpetuate it? In my case, a part of my Point A included believing, "I'm a piece of shit"; that story that I uncovered through this process, that I was constantly telling myself. Likewise, my client Nancy, and many others that I've helped over the years, were gripping tightly to that belief as a reason to stop living. In each case, the refocusing on a BIG Why, a purpose, and ultimately shifting the perspective of "what's wrong with me" instead to "what happened to me" helped.

To shift from "what's wrong with me" to "what happened to me," I suggest adding the question, "what's strong with me?" In other words, **what evidence of resilience have I already demonstrated?** What has worked to get me from where I was, in the midst of adversity, to where I am now? Evidence of proven resilience can be the very thing that gets us out of the depths of despair and outfits us with tools to face current adversity--and the inevitable adversity we'll face in the future. Because, you know, we're not pieces of shit, but shit happens.

CHAPTER TWO

Context: What Are ACEs and Toxic Stress?

When we finally let go of what no longer serves us, what we're holding, what we know, we make room to invite new wisdom, new choices, new freedom.

—*Tamara Levitt*

When ACEs proliferate, mental health deteriorates. Three in four adolescents experienced one ACE during the pandemic. Those adolescents were more likely to report mental health issues and suicidality (Anderson et al., 2022). ACEs affect physical health, mental health, social health and economic health. Understanding ACEs, and your own experience with them, is crucial for healing yourself and serving youth.

*　　*　　*

As I walked to the front of the meeting room of the community center to lead a presentation on the science and impact of Adverse Childhood Experiences (ACEs), I saw the men and women in the audience as children. I sensed the inner child in each one of them. More than a hundred teachers, child advocates, therapists, and clinical psychologists, all itching—craving—to learn how to help the children and youth in their care, how to break the cycle of neglect, abuse, and family dysfunction that most children in their care experience. The individuals who gravitate toward these helping professions, in most cases, have experienced their own childhood trauma. They're here on a mission.

After my presentation at the community center, Emma, a twenty-five-year-old elementary school teacher, came up to me. Her sandy hair was in a messy bun. She wore no jewelry except a silver watch on her left wrist. Thick, black mascara coated her lashes, hiding her emerald-green eyes. There were dark circles underneath them.

"Can I just send my kids to you?" she laughed. Her smile was infectious. She made eye contact, and I could see her pain. I suspected it was rooted in the past.

"Listen, so my dad...Gosh, I can't believe I'm getting emotional about this...it was so long ago..." A tiny tear trickled down her tortoise-shell glasses. She brushed it off nonchalantly.

She apologized for her emotions, as most often do. I remained silent, letting her sit with the sensations and figure out what she wanted to say to me next.

"My parents got divorced. I lost the stability of my home. We moved around from place to place, wherever we could stay. Sometimes in garages, a whole family with my sister and brother, all in one room. We were hungry too. A lot. And I lost my dad. He was the one who kicked us out."

We stood there for a moment, hearing footsteps from other audience members trekking towards the door. I thought about what I wanted to say to her. I felt compelled to help her at that moment. Sometimes the topic of this presentation brings up feelings. That's why there are resources available to assist in processing the information presented. But Emma needed someone to listen. I listened.

Soon, her green eyes lit up, and I saw a new spark within her. A fire. A light at the end of a tunnel.

"You know what stood out for me today?" she asked. "I did what I had to do, and I'm not proud of all of the decisions I made as a teenager and a young adult, Lorry...but being here today, recognizing that I had eight ACEs like you, and all of mine were before the age of seven years old...I guess I didn't realize how my past could be connected to my present life and my decision to be a teacher. Only, I recognize when students come to school hungry, and I always make sure I have snacks for them to eat. I remember how that felt, showing up in the same stained T-shirt, day after day, my hair dirty, stomach growling. Sometimes I was so hungry I couldn't even concentrate. I want to be an advocate for my past self. I want to be an advocate for my students. I have kids who remind me of what I went through, unfortunately. No kid should show up to school hungry and miserable."

Emma exhaled, taking a slow, deep breath, shuddering, remembering how she felt eighteen years ago.

*   *   *

ACEs are Adverse Childhood Experiences, that occur in childhood (birth to seventeen years old), according to the original CDC-Kaiser Permanente Adverse Childhood Experiences Study, or ACE Study CDC which took place between 1995 and 1998. The ACE Study is the largest public health study of its kind. More than 17,000 health maintenance organization members from Southern California completed confidential surveys. Almost two-thirds of study participants reported at least one ACE, and more than one in five reported three or more ACEs. The ACE Study investigated the connection between child abuse, neglect, and household dysfunctions, and physical, mental health, and societal outcomes.

A child's environment is critical to development. If a child grows up with caregivers who experience substance misuse, mental health issues, or instability due to parental separation, for example, development is compromised. In fact, those specific ACEs are identified in the landmark ACE study.

Sadly, Emma wasn't the only person in the room with numerous ACEs. In fact, like other audiences of youth-serving professionals and leaders, roughly 35 percent of the room (according to their sheets of paper they slipped to me during the break) had four or more, and only 15 percent had zero ACEs.

Of course, the ACEs count is only part of the picture. The most striking thing to me about the original ACE study is that not any one ACE appeared to be any more predictive of future risk than another. For example, it did not appear to indicate that any type of abuse was predictive of future risk than having an alcoholic parent. That seemed counterintuitive to me. Instead, the level of repeated exposure to stress, without buffering supports, seems to be a predictive factor. Exposure to toxic stress associated with these specific adversities is linked to higher risk of chronic health problems, mental illness, and substance use problems in adulthood. ACEs and the accompanying toxic stress can negatively impact education, job opportunities, earning potential, and financial difficulties. The more ACEs an individual has, the higher their exposure to toxic stress--and the lower their life expectancy, as well as the more likely they are to see lasting health consequences. ACEs are linked to specific chronic health issues, such as diabetes, cancer, and/or high blood pressure, as well as mental health issues, such as anxiety, depression, PTSD, and suicide. Now, mental health professionals are also studying other related adverse life experiences -- including food insecurity, forced separation, racism, caregiver disability, and community violence, and more--and how they impact someone's level of toxic stress.

Roughly twenty-four years into my work as a psychologist, I watched Dr. Nadine Burke Harris's 2014 TEDMED Talk, "How Childhood Trauma Affects Health Across a Lifetime." In her presentation, she discusses the connection between ACEs and the risk of physical and mental health problems in both children and adults. According to the Centers for Disease Control and Prevention (CDC), about 61 percent of adults surveyed across twenty-five states reported that they'd experienced at least one type of adverse childhood experience. Nearly one in five reported they'd experienced four or more types of ACEs. ACEs are common. They're everywhere. But they don't have to alter your future. Just because you've experienced ACEs in your past does not mean they have to make up your future.

*   *   *

When I first learned about the impact of ACEs, I began to talk with education professionals and teachers, student teachers, students studying psychology, counseling, and social work. I felt, and still feel, it's in their professional interest to know and understand how their own lives—especially their own childhoods—can negatively or positively affect their work and affect the children they are serving. Echoing Emma, many teachers I've spoken with over the years feel they need to be mental health professionals as well as teachers because of the ways students are showing up in the classroom. By being the best version of yourself, you can learn exactly how to help your clients, students, and even peers be the best version of themselves in return.

Mindset Shift: I am learning how to be the best version of myself.

A more recent example of adversity in our lives was the 2020 Covid-19 pandemic. As a society, we experienced collective trauma: loss of loved ones, social isolation, loss of income, loss of traditions, celebrations, rites of passage, etc. Your high school neighbor's and/or students' senior prom was canceled. In-person graduations became live movies on computer screens, creating completely new, and some would say isolating, experiences. Fifteenth and fiftieth birthday parties were canceled. Family vacations were postponed. The loss of traditions, celebrations, and major milestones disrupted our lives, creating adversity, and, in some cases, trauma.

Pouring myself into ACEs research, I saw what happens when you experience adversity in childhood. ACEs can be passed down to the next generation, genetically and experientially. When I was in private practice as a psychologist, I saw my adult clients physically contract, unable to speak of horrific events they experienced at a young age--some before the age of three. They served as a clear mirror for my own experiences. I, too, tended to contract, physically and emotionally, sometimes curling up in a ball when thinking about the abuse, neglect, and violence I experienced by the time I was eighteen years old.

Mindset Shift: I willingly face my adversities.

According to Harvard University's Center on the Developing Child, a toxic stress response is when a child experiences "strong, frequent, and/or prolonged adversity—such as physical or emotional abuse, chronic neglect, caregiver substance abuse or mental illness, exposure to violence, and much more—all without support from beloved adults."

All the work I do is centered around reducing the negative impact of childhood adversity and trauma. My leadership roles were and are aimed at breaking the cycle in the next generation, and I continue to emphasize the necessity to use proven strategies that build resilience and address the impact of the toxic stress response caused by exposure to childhood adversity.

Deep in my soul, I knew it was critically important to heal my own wounds in order to help others heal. I became passionate about helping people who had previously experienced ACEs, including myself, to build resilience for the purpose of radically shifting the trajectory of the next generation of children who had faced adversity, by first mastering resilience in our own circumstances. I also knew the importance of intentionally building in buffers for these children to prevent ACEs and the toxic stress of other adverse experiences from happening in the first place.

In 1942, my maternal grandmother divorced her husband. It was unheard of during that time for a woman to be on her own. My mother was only three years old, and her trajectory included alcoholism and multiple marriages, the first one at the age of fifteen. Unfortunately, her trajectory was predictable because of her exposure to childhood trauma in the first three years of life.

My own chaotic childhood was far from perfect. For any semblance of constancy, I thank the teachers I found along the way who believed in me wholeheartedly. My second-grade teacher saw my intrinsic value. She could've seen my talking out of turn in class as a discipline problem, grounds to be sent to the principal's office. She could've scolded me in front of others, which was common for teachers to do. Instead, she nurtured my strengths and believed in me. In sixth grade, Mr. Brown saw my troubled mind yet decided to help me stay on course, always giving me extra math worksheets and sending me to the lunch tables to do more advanced work independently rather than risk having me disrupt the class. Toward the end of the school year, he sent me outside of the classroom with a statistics workbook, a deck of cards, and some dice to learn probability and statistics along with another student. In college, Sister Helen Franklin served the same purpose. These teachers believed in me, perhaps more than I believed in myself. They treasured my personality and led me to see how I could be valuable in society. They provided me strength when I had none to give myself, no matter what crisis or challenge I came across. I came to realize an important factor in my healing journey, Hope. It's part of my purpose to empower other leaders and influencers of children and youth to do the same.

Studying ACEs spawned even more questions about my own childhood and how I could potentially help others. What if my grandmother had known about the intergenerational impact of childhood trauma? What if she knew what we know now? What if she came to realize how her decisions would impact future generations in my family? What if my mom had known? Though having ACEs are not a life sentence, I have hope for future generations in the face of dealing with adversities. Unfortunately, in the case of my mom and grandmother, their ACEs trapped them in a life of constant struggle and adversity. In my mom's case, no one knew about ACEs. My mom endured alcoholism along with mental health issues and had multiple marriages (her fifth when I was in college). Research shows that when children are exposed to repeated adversity with no buffering, the toxic stress response goes wild. In fact, children's brain chemicals are physiologically altered, developing in a very different pattern after experiencing adversity.

My mom didn't have the resources or the knowledge to understand how her alcoholism and marriages impacted me. I initially blamed her and these circumstances for the reckless, self-destructive decisions I made as a teenager and young adult. What kind of self-destructive decisions? Riding a bus through inner city San Diego to give up my virginity to a stranger I'd met through a hookup line (it was a decision to give it away rather than have it taken from me), doing drugs, sneaking out at night before I could drive, putting myself in harmful relationships—the list goes on. Now I take complete responsibility for my decisions, but for many years I held onto deep anger. It's taken me decades to accept that my mother didn't have the access to mental health care that I did (and still do). She didn't even go to therapy until she was nearing retirement age.

**Mindset Shift: Though I cannot change my past,
I can change my future.**

Yes, I had regrets. Yes, I've made mistakes in my life. Yet, I no longer focus on those. My teachers, mentors, therapists, and coaches, and the work I've done for more than thirty years, now as a psychologist and a leader in the field of children's mental health, have helped me realize that I have control of my own life, and it's okay that I didn't have control over my life earlier, or my grandmother's or my mom's decisions. **I have control over the choices I make to help me achieve my goals.** I've forgiven my past self for the mistakes I made, for the choices I made that were self-destructive. I promised myself a long time ago that I would help other young people come to the same peace, in the face of their decisions that they say are mistakes.

When we discover toxins in our food, mold in our walls, or asbestos in the ceiling, we do everything we can do to get rid of these toxins. The same approach is required when we realize we and others have been exposed to toxic stress. I firmly believe that if a child is exposed to toxic levels of stress, we have a responsibility to buffer the toxicity by reducing or even eliminating those stressors from children's lives.

*   *   *

"Emma," I said, with deep compassion and understanding. I was still noticing those dark circles under her eyes. "Your vulnerability and experiences have helped make you the compassionate teacher you are today…How do you take care of yourself?"

"I've always felt this great sense that knowledge is power. This knowledge that you've given me here today has made me even more motivated and inspired to become a better leader and a better teacher to my kids…and to take care of myself better," she replied.

"I love that my presentation helped you think this way, Emma. Have you also considered what it means to care for yourself? It seems like you chose teaching because you want to help others who are going through what you went through."

She nodded vigorously.

"When we go on airplanes, you know how the flight attendants tell us to put our oxygen masks on first before helping others?"

"Yes, of course," Emma said. She knew where I was going.

"We must give ourselves air in order to be able to give others a part of ourselves. **We help ourselves so we can help others.** When we put others' well-being first, when we help the other passengers before ourselves, we sometimes feed a false sense of humility in our minds. It appears to be a very humble thing to serve others first, especially for the sake of the children. Like I said today, when we tell the world, 'I'm here to serve others,' it's important to learn what serving yourself means too. Being the best version of yourself is the best way you can give your all to the young people in your care."

Emma's expression froze as the realization hit. I've seen this expression countless times, but it was especially apparent during our conversation. For the first time, she understood why she chose teaching as her profession. She didn't only want to help the next generation succeed; she desperately needed to do so. Yet, she hadn't seemed to factor in that taking care of herself and her needs would be just as important as taking care of her students and theirs.

She opened her blue spiral notebook and turned to her notes from the presentation and began writing. She made a list then and there of ways she could take care of herself. Making time for yourself is critically important on this journey of healing and mastering resilience.

Mindset Shift: I get to make time to care for myself.

"I'm going to go outside in nature more. I'm going to set a time each day, for at least ten minutes, to pause and take deep breaths, and I'm going to schedule time each week to call one of my true friends."

I smiled, pleased that she remembered items on the list of self-care options I'd shared during my presentation. She seemed satisfied. I wondered if this would be the only interaction I had with her. That's common in my work, and, frankly, it can be a little jolting––meeting someone's singular personality, along with their keenest vulnerabilities, and then, at the end of a talk or workshop, having to say good-bye. Still, I felt comfort in believing Emma had a transformative experience from the presentation and our discussion. I know from personal experience that just one interaction has the potential to change the trajectory of someone's journey.

*   *   *

If you want to truly understand the risk factors attributable to ACEs keep reading. Though not one of the official ingredients of Mastering Resilience, knowing the impact of ACEs specifically, provides the context for the importance of applying the ingredients to your healing journey. The experiences I had and decisions I made throughout my childhood and adulthood were predictable based on knowing the science of ACEs and what they do to the developing brains and bodies of young children and the illness, behaviors, social determinants of health, and precursors to mental unwellness. The types of choices I made, the illnesses I had, things that happened to me, and that I did to myself are all highlighted as risks in the ACEs literature. And also, keep reading if you want to hear the stories of hope that come from mastering resilience. By truly understanding the science behind ACEs, I believe future ACEs can be prevented. Generational cycles can be broken. To truly come along this healing journey with me, I want you to first acknowledge your ACEs score (www.numberstory.org) and other adversities in your life. Ignoring these critical pieces will be detrimental to your overall healing journey. By reintroducing your past to your present self in a new way, you'll soon be able to heal more deeply, incorporating that knowledge into the work you do with students or children.

Providing trauma-informed care to children and families gives me great joy and satisfaction. My goal is to move the needle from one in five children being diagnosed with a mental disorder to one in ten children in this generation. I now call myself a master of resilience, a thriver of childhood adversity--not a survivor or a victim. I lead other professionals in this manner too.

CHAPTER THREE

Commitment

The biggest commitment you must keep is your commitment to yourself.

—*Neale Donald Walsch*

Becoming a mentor or a positive role model for young people is one way to positively impact youth mental health. According to a recent study in *Nature*, "Adolescents need healthy relationships with parents and other adults; these are essential for young people's mental health and well-being" (Fulgini & Galván, 2022). Being part of a healthy relationship means forging a healthy relationship with yourself.

*   *   *

The second ingredient of Mastering Resilience is Commitment. It's critically important for you to make the *decision* to commit to your own healing. Some say that to create the optimal conditions for your commitment, you must establish a BIG Why. Reread chapter one if you want a refresh on the concept of the BIG Why.

To make the BIG Why actionable at this moment in time, you get to establish your Why NOW.

*   *   *

"I wish you had healed from your trauma before you had children," my twenty-something child once told me.

"I thought I had," was my only response.

I remembered all the emotional work I had done. When I was in my early thirties, before I had children, at one of my weekly Thursday sessions with my therapist at the time, Dr. Jane, I was expressing my frustrations and adversities I was facing at that time in my life.

"Jane, I'm so upset that Gary and I are having these infertility issues. I thought I would be pregnant again by now."

Getting pregnant wasn't the problem; staying pregnant was. I'd had two miscarriages around the time of the first year of marriage, and two more later, losses that shook us. Gary and I had decided to wait a little while before trying again, only then it seemed we couldn't get pregnant.

"Why is this happening to me?" I asked Dr. Jane. I felt desperate and pitiful. I felt very "poor me."

Little did I know that behind this question lay hundreds of unsolved mysteries within my past. I recognized I had many wounds, but their effects on my present state of mind or being were entirely invisible to me. I spent so much time reliving past adversities, let alone current ones. Though I wasn't completely distraught in this therapy session, I was having a mini pity party. In an earlier session, Dr. Jane had said to me, "You're putting your own adversities in a trophy case, like you are really proud of them." My victim mentality shifted in that instant. I thought

I had been resilient, and to some extent I was. I was a resilient victim. I was so resilient that I was displaying my own adversities, wearing them like a badge of honor, showcasing how I'd been a victim of my circumstances rather than how I had taken steps to heal myself so I could help others. She didn't have to remind me of the trophy case.

"I realize I'm looking forward to a larger breakthrough," I said at our next session. Then I told Dr. Jane about an upcoming women's retreat I'd been invited to by my friend, Michelle.

I again had been looking for fellowship with women, for spiritual guidance that this time would provide support and encouragement for me during this time of sadness. I consider myself to be a spiritual person, connected to what I choose to call God. Others might refer to it as connecting to a higher power, the divine, source, the universe, the be all and end all, or personal power. I was seeking guidance from something greater than myself to help me understand my purpose and that could help me put my current suffering in context.

"Lorry, I think this retreat will be really, really great for you," Dr. Jane said, writing notes on her legal pad. I wondered how many legal pads worth of my life she had in my file; I'd been going to her weekly for five years now. "I know your spirituality is important to you, and it's ultimately your own spiritual journey as you dig deeper to recognize how these wounds and scars of your past impact your beliefs today, Lorry. What do you think is underlying these feelings?" She had permission to deal with my analytic side. I responded something superficial since it was all I could do. Then she asked, "What steps can you take to truly feel blessed and grateful?"

Several moments passed before I could answer this one. My mind was churning. She'd hit the nail on the head. For some reason, I hadn't truly recognized the victim mentality that remained all these years: the "poor me" mentality; the "something's wrong with me" mentality; the "why does everything bad always happen to me?" mentality; the "I can't seem to catch a break" mentality.

Finally, I lifted my head and looked at her. "I care so much about making a difference in my work and in my life that I always think of others first. I don't ever seem to think of myself, my needs or wants or likes/dislikes or anything else about me. It's always about someone else."

Dr. Jane put down her pen and took off her glasses, staring at me.

"Lorry, be gentler with yourself. Cut yourself some slack. Pay more attention to taking care of yourself. By doing so, you'll not only help yourself, but you'll have more fuel in your tank to help more people discover who they truly are too."

When I walked out of her office that day, I was ready for the retreat. I was ready to learn more about myself for the first time in a long, long time. It was at that retreat where I learned to put a stake in the ground to represent a firm commitment to my healing journey. Literally, I drove a stake into the earth. One day, the facilitators passed out small brown wooden stakes, carefully shaped to easily drive into the soil of our choice. We each received one to take home with us with instructions to find a place in our yards, or a pot full of soil, to pound the stake in the ground, representing the commitment we made to our healing journey. This stake would mark a place that we could revisit time and time again to remind us to visualize the day we made that commitment and recommit if needed to the ongoing process of our healing. What was my Why NOW at that time? I no longer wanted to go through my life with a victim mentality. Even though I'd garnered some level of success in my life and career up to that point, it was clear that the "poor me" attitude was running the show.

I had my youngest child shortly after my fortieth birthday and long after I drove that stake in the ground, signifying the lasting commitment to my healing journey.

"Mommy, is there a God?" the same inquisitive child asked when she was much younger. She was young enough to be strapped in a car seat in the back of our Black Isuzu Trooper on the way down to San Diego to see my family for our traditional Christmas Eve gathering.

"I'd like to think so," I said, wondering what was going on in her mind.

"Why would God put you in a family where your mom ripped your lips off?" she said innocently.

My thoughts raced. *When did she hear that?!? Have I damaged her? I'm a horrible mother! She must have overheard me talking to someone.* "Ripping my lips off" was how I would describe the angry interactions with my mother that occurred in the past. My mother had very long, curved acrylic nails. Claws. When I attempted to speak my mind, she would grab my lips with her nails and scream, "Don't you talk back to me!"

The answer to my child's questions came like a divine download. "Well, Mommy's work is to help children who have been hurt, who need help, and Mommy knows what that's like because of the things that happened to her. So, she knows how to help them."

"Oh." Thankfully, she was satisfied with my answer.

Each year, the interactions and experiences with my children seemed to draw out insecurities and fears that I would be just like my mom, and along with that came multiple opportunities to assess my Why NOW. Even when I thought I had healed, I was reminded again and again that healing is a process. Each step of the journey involved a decision, a series of opportunities to commit to my healing.

Your Why NOW can change and evolve over time. In other words, the reason and motivation for your lasting commitment can change. Many of my reasons were related to my close relationships, my parenting, my work style, etc. Why NOW? At one point for me, it was because I wanted to lose my victim mentality; at another, because I didn't want to ruin my marriage; at yet another, I looked back on my younger self and desperately wanted to help that seventeen-year-old girl.

Your commitment is simply a firm decision--a stake in the ground, if you will--to do what it takes to heal. The Why NOW is the motivation, at any given time, to keep going, to do whatever it takes to continue the healing journey. Whereas the BIG Why is the inspiration and the future state where success is the only option, where it can be described as your ideal state in the future, the Why NOW is the motivation, the commitment, the reason you made the decision to act now. That reason can change, but the decision is the same.

When you establish your Why NOW and continuously acknowledge your commitment to the healing process of Mastering Resilience, you get in touch with your intrinsic value-- and you may begin to behave differently toward yourself and the world around you. Even though you may have experienced childhood trauma and/or adversity, I want you to know that you're not alone, and that there's hope for you to become a master of resilience and help others do the same.

Hope can come from the teacher who believed in you. Hope can come from a long-ago interaction with a friend's uncle who happened to be a CASA worker. Perhaps you've known the loving touch of a nurse in a frightening time at the hospital or maybe it was the coach who drove you home after the game when no one was there to pick you up. You know what it feels like to have that caring, dependable adult who believed in you. And you know that's who

YOU are to the next generation. **Hope comes from knowing you can rewire your brain to engage in new ways of thinking, feeling, and behaving that better serve you and to break the cycle.**

Once you make the lasting commitment to your healing process and establish your Why NOW, you'll discover you possess the capacity to create a future based on loving yourself, a future where you're not afraid of showcasing your intrinsic value to the outside world.

*   *   *

In my weekly supervision times with my intern, Alex, we frequently discussed various expressions of commitment: commitment to treatment, commitment to healing, and what it really meant to commit to our own healing journey.

After reviewing his cases, he said, "I'm so motivated to help each and every one of my clients, Lorry. I take my work very seriously."

He combed his hands through his thick hair. He said he couldn't make the time for a haircut yet due to his classes and workload. I reassured him the length of his hair was not an issue. It was obvious he wanted to make a good impression. I made it my goal for him to be able to feel the unconditional acceptance from me, for him to know his intrinsic value, and the significance of the impact he was having on the children in his care.

"Lorry, you know I didn't get to have a mentor in my life until I met you," he smiled shyly, and I smiled back. "Now, I need to become the mentor to these kids that I never had as a child. That's the commitment I'm making."

I nodded, thinking about his statement.

"You GET to be their mentor," I said.

There's an important distinction between "get to be" and "need to be." "Needing" to do something implies feelings of obligation that we naturally resist whereas "getting" to do something suggests an opportunity, a special chance, even something positive you might look forward to. I often shared an example of shifting the language around picking up my children from separate after-school activities. We "*get* to pick up your sister now" versus "we *need* to pick up your sister now." That one little shift in the language completely recasts the same event.

He smiled as I spoke. It was clear he was putting the needs of others over his own needs at the expense of his self-care.

"Alex, have you considered what your commitment to your own well-being is at this point in your life?"

Alex sat expressionless. His hands fell to his lap, and he stared at me with his deep, brown eyes. Then he sighed with the weight of the world heavy on his shoulders. "I... well, to tell you the truth, not really, Lorry."

I reminded Alex of the importance of daily commitment to self-care practices as he contemplated his response.

**Mindset Shift: I commit to making positive changes
in my life.**

Alex nodded, digesting this other commitment.

I tried to elaborate. I make a point of sharing and/or modeling daily self-care practices, such as exercise, meditation, and expressing gratitude. "Do you see, though, how this commitment to myself doesn't necessarily have to do with my work? It has to do with how I prioritize things in my life, and how I choose to honor myself overall."

I spared him the details of my BIG Why and that my commitments big and small are a part of my overall Why NOW; I'm sure he's heard it more than once.

"Well, you've given me a lot to think about, Lorry. I don't want to keep you from your next meeting, so I'll mosey out of your office now, but I'll see you next week."

It was clear he would make a great therapist because his heart is in this line of work for the right reason, the children. I wondered just how similar Alex's BIG Why might be to mine. Was his purpose, like mine, breaking the cycle for the next generation? Fostering more positive, uplifting experiences for youth?

"Wait, Alex, before you go, please think about what I said. Let's talk about your commitment to yourself next week after we go through our cases."

He smiled again, and I saw his right dimple shine through. "Thanks, Lorry."

*   *   *

When Alex came into my office the following week, we spent more time discussing the topic of commitment.

"I spent a lot of time pondering what you asked me about last week, Lorry, and I think I came to a conclusion," he said. "I'm learning there are some boundaries I set up in advance. I also realized there are experiences I haven't dealt with yet, or worked through, from my own childhood that are negatively impacting my work life and my capacity to help these kids to the best of my ability. To be honest, I've done some of my own therapy work, as you know, but I think I need...*get* to do more reflection of my past, even though I know it might not be fun."

I nodded, happy that he had listened to our conversation and even happier that he'd taken it to heart.

"Have you thought about your Big WHY or your Why NOW, Alex?"

"Yes, I believe my Big WHY is the same as yours, Lorry. But now I realize that I have a responsibility to heal myself to break the cycle in the next generation. I don't want to perpetuate my past into their future."

I thought about what Alex said for a long while before responding. Today was the day he decided to commit to his own healing once and for all.

"Alex, I want you to buy a new calendar, and I want you to mark today's date on there with a big, red marker."

His black pen dropped onto the brown carpeted floor in my office just then, and he slowly picked it up.

"I think I only have black pens," he said, confirming what we both knew—that all charts needed to be signed with black ink.

"Here, take one of mine."

As I handed him one of my trusty favorites, I flashed back to a time when I was in Alex's shoes. Up to that point, I felt as though I had a lot of book knowledge and successful experiences with my own clients, yet I couldn't quite figure out which strategies to apply to fully heal myself. And though I had previously made prominent commitments in my life, I hadn't quite realized the importance of declaring the lasting commitment to my own healing journey, which meant doing whatever it takes to heal, namely, successfully identifying my purpose statement and my BIG Why. Understanding the critical nature of that first step came later. It was the day I drove that stake in the ground, the one I received at the women's retreat so many years earlier. It was then that I took control of my life and my own healing journey. I made a pledge. I made a commitment to breaking the cycle in the next generation. I know the importance of marking that day on the calendar and in the earth.

Of course, there are commitments small and large. I make commitments to practice daily self-care. I make a commitment to myself to be a better person today than I was yesterday. I also make big commitments. I never wanted to get divorced because of my upbringing, and because I experienced how my mom's marriages and divorces negatively affected me. I'm sure that's why I waited to get married until I was in my thirties. Before meeting my husband, Gary, I had a habit of pushing people away to avoid commitment. In fact, I had a whole playbook for avoiding commitment. Sometimes, I withdrew or withheld my feelings. Sometimes, I would just utter sounds, like "Ugh!" Not words, just sounds.

Yet, to this day, I'm still happily married, despite the ups and downs my husband and I have navigated together because of the commitment to work through whatever comes our way. We've stood by each other. The adversities we've faced together have served to make our bond stronger. The feeling of love has wavered at times, of course, but our commitment still holds strong. My wedding anniversary and the day I drove the stake in the ground are days I always remember.

I told Alex where my mind had been, and how he, too, could mark his calendar and take that next step on his healing journey. He felt like he'd reached a plateau, and he wanted a few extra tools to devise his healing plan. He had already established his BIG Why; it was time to make his specific commitments as his Why NOW.

*   *   *

Back when Dr. Jane told me I was putting my adversities in a trophy case, I realized I needed to have a larger breakthrough, and I would revisit that concept as time went on. And after the women's retreat, I was so ready to drive that little wooden stake into the dirt. I was ready for the ceremony. In fact, I was desperate for it, just like I was desperate to make a commitment to myself: to make being a victim a thing of the past; to begin my ultimate healing journey.

The Healing Pledge

Are you longing to commit to your healing once and for all? Are you ready to live on purpose and for a purpose? Are you ready to document your Why NOW?

In my course, Mastering Resilience, I walk students through their own healing pledge. Congratulations on deciding that today is your day to commit. After you've marked down today's date on your calendar, like Alex did, you'll create a pledge to yourself, and for yourself. This pledge is the first huge step you'll take to master resilience in your own life.

Remember, the definition of commitment is "an agreement or pledge to do something in the future." The definition of the "purpose" is "something set up as an object or end to be attained."

To break the cycle fully and completely, though, Alex chose to take his healing pledge during one of our meetings:

I, Alex, solemnly pledge to heal the hurts of my past, to take decisive action to create my desired life and my ideal future, and to step into my purpose with enthusiasm and excitement, so that I can be ALL that I am intended to BE.

This pledge is a solemn promise to yourself. It's a declaration of intentional self-love. Once you take this healing pledge like Alex, you'll be on the first step of your commitment to breaking the cycles and patterns that no longer serve you on your journey.

There may be setbacks along the way, but the rise and fall only proves your ultimate commitment to mastering resilience.

Like Alex, Emma, and myself, you may also want to break the cycle of abuse, neglect, or trauma for the next generation. I encourage you to commit to this healing process now so you, too, can have a greater impact on the young people in your care, and you truly will be able to break the cycle for the next generation. This is your greatest *why*, your incredible vision for your future and your work.

Remember, though, that to break the cycle, you get to commit fully to your healing journey and work to heal yourself. And step into your greater purpose. Your impact requires integrity. I firmly believe that you have a moral obligation to be a cycle breaker. You are here for a reason. To step into your greatness and to live in your purpose, you must heal. When you experience the freedom that comes from letting go of the past, other people around you gain the ability to do the same.

CHAPTER FOUR

Clarity of Self:
Who you think you are versus
who you really are

When things feel murky and unsure, fine-tuning
our hearing so as to distinguish the voice
of our Innermost Self brings clarity.

—Kristi Bowman

Cognitive distortions, which Dr. Peter Grinspoon defines as "internal mental filters or biases that increase our misery, fuel our anxiety, and make us feel bad about ourselves," pose problems for everyone, but especially for youth with ACEs. In a study of incarcerated adolescents in Sweden, researchers found that, "negative cognitive distortions were more prevalent in the juvenile delinquent population than in a control group," (Larden et al., 2006). No wonder understanding and taming our own cognitive distortions is imperative if we want to help youth in crisis.

*   *   *

In my twenties, I was on two roads––call one the Road to Self-Destruction and the other Straight-A-Student Road. My ultimate self-destruction felt like my truth; straight-A, a fraud. This duality surprised people who knew me on only one of the roads. My classmates couldn't believe how much I loved racing around helmetless on motorcycles at high speeds. The acquaintances who witnessed my self-destructive behavior couldn't believe I was a straight-A student in graduate school.

I grew up in a house rife with alcohol abuse and violence. Multiple marriages meant multiple dads, and lots of yelling and screaming, chaos, and fear. I learned to sleep with a pillow over my head to drown out the noise. But that didn't stop me from internalizing the hateful words I'd heard over and over: "You're rotten, you're stupid, you're fat, you're a cry baby. I wish you had never been born!"

Certainly, the risk factors were present to have a really bad outcome.

I chose to numb my feelings with drugs, to look for love through sex; I had a death wish. I couldn't stand the constant feelings of inadequacy, rejection, brokenheartedness, sadness, worry, and shame. I carried so much shame. The shame I felt about the traumatic events paled in comparison to the shame I felt about my own choices. Day in and day out. I believed my true self was the Lorry making poor choices––very risky, self-destructive choices.

The Lorry who was a straight-A student her first semester at UCLA? She was a fake.

I judged myself harshly for the choices I made, and I believed the sum of my choices made me an inherently bad person. I also found it nearly impossible to acknowledge my accomplishments. In fact, as I would meet one goal, I would set another one, without taking a moment to celebrate. I never felt good enough.

I was always striving for perfection on an elusive journey toward acceptance.

*   *   *

We are born whole and pure. Babies are intrinsically good. They don't know positive or negative thoughts. Babies are beautiful, and parents say frequently that babies can't do anything wrong—they eat, sleep, cry, and poop. All in all, it's a simple existence. As we grow up, we're told that we can do anything we set our minds to--at least, some of us are told this. Not everybody hears these affirmative words.

Instead, adults who've experienced ACEs (Alex, Emma, me) were told negative comments by those we trusted. We believed what we heard, and we molded and shaped those beliefs inside ourselves. In fact, those experiences and words we heard as children and young adults form the basis of our false self-identities.

It's *critical* to start paying attention to the words you use about yourself. When I first started listening to what I was telling myself about myself, I was astounded. How could one person have so many condemning thoughts seemingly simultaneously? I made a game of it. Once I counted more than ten condemning conscious thoughts at the same time—ten horrible things I was telling myself all at once. That didn't include the subconscious ones.

Your negative, conscious and subconscious thoughts have molded your self-image and continue to damage your self-esteem, and, most dangerously, they can impose themselves on your identity and shape what you believe about who you are. Not only that, but they also have implications for your physical and mental health.

In his book *Chatter,* Dr. Ethan Kross, a prominent psychologist, professor, and the director of the Emotion & Self Control Laboratory at the University of Michigan, writes:

> One of the most chilling discoveries I've had in my career is that (mental) chatter doesn't simply hurt people in an emotional sense; it has physical implications for our body as well, from the way we experience physical pain all the way down to the way our genes operate in our cells...Chronic negative thoughts can also push into the territory of mental illness, though this isn't to say chatter is the same thing as clinical depression, anxiety, or post-traumatic stress disorder. Repetitive negative thinking isn't synonymous with these conditions, but it's a common feature of them.

Dr. Kross goes on to say that the most frightening part is how chatter can affect our health and feed our stress levels. "When our panic response is prolonged, the gradual physiological erosion it causes can harm more than our ability to fight sickness and keep our body running smoothly. It can change the way our DNA influences our health."

Perhaps this is why I'm so committed to helping others cultivate the ability to speak to themselves with loving- kindness. I want people to truly love themselves. Not in a selfish or self-serving way, but in a genuine self-honoring way, one in which we model for others to do the same. Other people in our lives, especially children, pick up on our patterns of self-hatred and loathing. When we gain clarity about ourselves, acknowledge our intrinsic value, and accept our own unique qualities, it inspires children, youth, and others in our circle of influence to be the best versions of themselves. We owe it to ourselves (and to them) to get really clear about who we are, what our value is, how we manifest our unique brilliance (a term used by Fabienne Fredrickson that signifies "things you do that energize you, that make your heart sing"), and what comprises our purpose in this world.

So, what exactly is the next ingredient of the recipe for mastering resilience: Clarity of Self? Clarity of self is being sure about:

> your intrinsic value;
>
> what you like;
>
> what you don't like;
>
> your values;
>
> your talents and abilities;
>
> your character; and
>
> your setbacks or limitations, i.e., the things you find challenging.

Knowing ourselves, our preferences, and tendencies in all these categories allows us to have a clear picture of the person we are. Clarity of self is a key ingredient to Mastering Resilience and moving along on this healing journey. Remember our cake analogy? Clarity is the egg you're whipping with a whisk. That egg will bind everything together.

*   *   *

To have clarity of self, first you must recognize that you have intrinsic value. Though this sounds simple, for adults who've experienced ACEs, this may not come naturally.

What is intrinsic value? Intrinsic value is your inherent worth. Value is inherent in your very existence. You have value because you exist. In philosophy, intrinsic value is the value that something has "for its own sake," as opposed to being valuable "for the sake of something else." Knowing your own intrinsic value is the foundation of your identity--it feeds into your True Self.

We can characterize our True Self using "I am" statements. For example:

I am a compassionate person who sees the good in people.

I am a bright light that ignites the spark in people that fuels their confidence.

I am a loyal spouse.

I am a great parent.

I am a vessel of love designed to help heal the brokenhearted.

I am brilliant.

I am strong.

I am independent.

I am a healer.

I am a warrior.

I am resilient.

Living as our True Selves, and being the best version of ourselves, means knowing who we really are--and believing in our intrinsic value. You might say, "I am uniquely designed" or "I am fearfully and wonderfully made." You might say, "I'm here for a reason that only I can fulfill" or "I have value because I am me." No matter what words you use, you are acknowledging your gifts, your talents, and your presence--the fact that you're a valuable contributor to society. Perhaps you like to dance, to sing, or to read. You know your values and what you value in life, as well as what's important to you. You recognize your talents, abilities, and the qualities of your character. You may just know what you don't like, and that's a start.

Part of the reason that clarity of self is so important for resilience is because knowing your true identity and taking actions consistent with that identity supercharges your healing journey! As you add more ingredients to the Mastering Resilience process, you'll see how knowing ourselves, our unique qualities, and having clarity of self, connects to our feelings, thoughts, and beliefs, and why that *self-knowledge* will be the catalyst to creating our ideal future state.

When we have clarity of self, it's easier for us to express our needs in ways that make it more likely to get them met. We can also use this knowledge to make sure that we are taking care of ourselves. Self-care is critical. Think of it as a personal "love language." When we know our likes and dislikes, we can refuel in ways that make all the difference in the world. When we have clarity around our likes and dislikes, it's easier to gauge whether our choices will move us closer to our ultimate goals. And when we know our setbacks, our triggers, and the things that cause us to question our True Selves, we can make a conscious effort to avoid those things and not allow them to invade our lives.

Mindset Shift: Clarity allows us to be more consistent.

Often, when we're not living out our true potential, it's because we don't trust ourselves to always make decisions in our own best interest. This is where our values come in. When we're behaving consistently with our values, we learn to trust ourselves more. We also recognize whether those around us are also doing the same. When we're behaving consistently with our values, we're more open and transparent with those around us--and they feel free to be the same.

Clarity allows us to be laser-focused. When we're laser-focused, it's easier to be resourceful when we hit obstacles in our path. Obstacles aren't permanent roadblocks, but rather places where we can course correct and calibrate to stay consistent with who we are.

Clarity of self also allows you to acknowledge your WORTH.

When you describe yourself through your qualities and characteristics, you feel better about yourself. And when you deeply acknowledge your intrinsic value, no mistake, no bad decision, and no adversity can detract from you. Mistakes are opportunities for learning; so are successes. The value we have intrinsically isn't determined by any of that. That's really good news for us.

The clearer we are about who we are, the easier it is to make sense of circumstances outside of ourselves.

Once you have clarity of self, you can counteract negative thinking like never before. When you catch yourself thinking hateful words spoken to you by others (or to yourself about yourself), it's possible to *choose* to think of encouraging words instead; the sooner the better. Words are powerful to your psyche. They form your core beliefs and the perception of your identity, which is what impacts what you believe about your intrinsic value. What we tell ourselves illuminates what we believe about ourselves, and this dictates how we behave. Our perceived identity impacts our choices, how we spend our time, who we choose as our friends, our jobs, our income, and more. Not only is it important for us to unveil what we believe, we also must reveal the underlying feelings too.

The words we tell ourselves create what's in our hearts. Harsh words create cruelty and anger, triggering feelings of impatience, ungratefulness, sadness, anxiety, and fear. Enthusiastic, encouraging words create love and positivity, which activate feelings like spirituality, kindness, humility, love, forgiveness, and grace. Lasting change in beliefs and behavior only happens when we become aware of the feelings we hold and when we honor them. There needs to be an established emotional connection. After all, emotion is the ignition switch that sparks action.

The publications about how many words we think a day varies from a few thousand to tens of thousands. For the sake of this example, let's assume it's on the lower end. According to a recent study in *Nature Communication*, the average person has 6,200 thoughts per day, many of which are negative and repetitive. So having negative thoughts is normal and automatic, which is why it's important to be intentional about interrupting them and replacing them with positive statements. As you start paying attention to the words you tell yourself about yourself, remember that those negative things you are saying to yourself have molded your self-image, damaged your self-esteem, and created your identity--in short, what you believe about who you ARE.

One of the first ways I learned to counteract negative thoughts was by adding more positive thoughts. My business coach, Fabienne Fredrickson, borrows this strategy from her earlier experience as a health coach. As Fabienne explained to me, "Think of what happens when a person decides to eat healthier. It's not realistic to banish potato chips and cookies and candy--that's not sustainable. You don't have to start by eliminating anything. Just put more good stuff on your plate and keep adding more good stuff. Eventually the bad stuff won't have any room on the plate." The same holds for positive thoughts. Think five positive thoughts for every one negative, and over time, it will get easier. You'll gain more clarity about your intrinsic value, your unique qualities and characteristics, your likes and dislikes. The more research I did about the power of words, I came to this conclusion: If you knew the power of your thoughts, you would do the work to never have another negative thought again.

Allow yourself the experience of internalizing your own "I am" statements. *I am kind.* Think of a time you demonstrated kindness to others. Feel the enjoyment of being kind. *I am strong.* Think of a time when you showed strength--physical strength or strength of character. Imagine that feeling of strength. *I am courageous.* What did you feel, taste, smell, and experience in that moment of courage? Allow yourself to imagine, feel, and experience your "I am" statements. Let it sink in.

*   *   *

Shortly after the conference where I met Emma, she asked me out for coffee. We began talking regularly, and one afternoon, she confided that she'd recently started dating again. On her last date, she was asked what her favorite hobby was, as well as her favorite color. She didn't have an answer.

"He tilted his head and looked at me sideways," she sighed. "He was like, 'How do you not know what your favorite color is? How do you not know that about yourself?' Is this normal, Lorry? I mean, I don't even know what my own likes and dislikes are. Over the years, I've been so focused on school, getting a job, and doing well at my job that my own hobbies have gone to the wayside. I don't think I'll go out with that guy again, but he did make me really think about who I am as a person."

I took a sip of my dark roast and turned toward her.

"Funny enough, this is incredibly common," I said. She asked me to elaborate. "I went through this same process when Gary built our house many years ago with his own two hands. He did a beautiful job. After the walls were up and it was time to decorate, I remember staring at the blank walls. I had absolutely no idea what I wanted to do with the empty space. I didn't even know what kind of design I liked. I remember walking into an interior design store in Laguna Niguel and the lady at the register rattled off some choices and asked me if I liked Art Deco, Minimalism, Bohemian, Mid-Century Modern, Victorian, Rustic, or Farmhouse. I was trying to imagine what on earth she was referring to. I was overwhelmed and found myself drowning in ideas as I looked around the huge showroom. All I wanted to do was go home and lie down on the cement floor--the big, uncarpeted space in the living room. We hadn't even bought a couch. The sales lady must've seen my confusion. She took me by the arm, guiding me towards different selections. I'm still, to this day, grateful for her. The process was long and a bit grueling, but at the end of it all, I figured out my own style at thirty-seven years old. In the years to come, I discovered that all I wanted was our children's artwork framed on the walls, along with family pictures hanging all around me. I even learned that my favorite color was purple. Like you, Emma, I never thought about asking myself what my favorite color was."

Emma jotted down a few notes in her small, red notebook with a pink pen.

"You know what, Lorry?" Emma stared at her pen for a moment. "I think my favorite color is pink."

It can be that simple. Having clarity of self doesn't have to be a big revelation. Just remember to be kind; we only have control over what we tell ourselves. Remember that the kinder you are to yourself, the more nourishing you can become to yourself.

When you have a clearer idea of your own intrinsic value and how your mental chatter affects your goals, you'll be on your way to mastering resilience. Clarity of self is a key concept to grasp along your individualized healing journey.

CHAPTER FIVE

Cognitive Consistency: the AAAs of Mastering resilience

*Courage is the most important of all the virtues
because without courage, you can't practice
any other virtue consistently.*

—*Maya Angelou*

Between 2009 and 2019, major depressive episodes in US youth increased by 7.7 percentage points (Daly, 2022). As mental health issues surge in children and adolescents, it's more important than ever for adults to step in and support positive interventions. The stakes are high. As University of Oxford psychiatrist William Kukyen puts it, "It's not just about preventing mental-health problems in children. It's about setting people up for life."

*   *   *

That second women's retreat I attended was a significant event in my life. Not only did I make a commitment about my healing journey, but I resolved to form habits that would effectively help me be the best version of myself.

At that retreat, a new friend, Sally, approached me wearing a bright colored, fitted, and slightly above-the-knee dress, with a rounded neckline and short sleeves. She offhandedly said, "You're wearing that?"

I looked down at my clothes: loose jeans, a hooded sweatshirt. Instantly, I took Sally's words as criticism. The inner dialog ramped up: *What's wrong with what I'm wearing? Does this make my butt look big? Should I be wearing a dress? Does she think my outfit is ugly?* and so on. Her brief comment occupied my thoughts the entire day. Soon, though, I realized that what seemed insignificant set off a chain of thoughts that penetrated to the core of my own belief systems, and what I believed to be who I truly was. It didn't occur to me at the time that I could say to myself, "So what if she doesn't like it?" or "What she thinks of me is none of my business." Maybe she appreciated that I could pull off jeans and a sweatshirt when she felt it was necessary to wear a dress. The point was, I immediately heard criticism from a person I'd just met. And I let that criticism influence my day--and my perception of myself.

I'm not the only one who has been there. The inner critic is alive and well fed. Fortunately, we can learn hacks to mitigate this collateral impact of verbal abuse or bullying, and/or internalizing things that have been said to you.

In the past, if I was criticized for anything, even a wardrobe choice, it would send off a chain of ruminating thoughts about everything I'd done wrong—not only that day, but my entire life. Choices I made in college. Choices I made as a teenager. My mother once asked me, "How can you be so smart in school and so dumb at home?" From there on, any bad choice I made resulted in me feeling and perceiving myself as dumb. Forget the fact that I routinely aced exams. If I got a 99 percent, I focused on the 1 percent I got wrong.

Negativity infected my internal rhetoric. I allowed myself to be in this negative headspace, and these critical voices became a part of my inner dialog. I felt completely unworthy of attaining anything more than I already had. It wasn't until much later in my life, and after years being on my healing journey, that I realized I could choose to make new agreements with myself. I realized that I was the only one in charge of my own belief system.

Mindset Shift: I alone am in control and in charge of my thoughts and perspectives.

Emma once shared with me that as a child she was told her hair was disgusting. Being raised by a single mom, (and exposed to multiple ACEs), often meant going without anything that wasn't a necessity. Shampoo was considered a luxury item. She, too, ruminated on this, and as an adult, she hated her hair. The words that adults spoke to her stayed with her. The spoken expressions children hear from others, especially words from authority figures like parents, teachers, and counselors, stick. These adults might be the very ones who intentionally or inadvertently say negative things that give life to our inner critics. These adults may not have a clue how these words will affect the children later in life.

If you have blonde hair and blue eyes, and someone insisted that you had dark, brown hair and green eyes, what would you say? What if they say it emphatically, with conviction, very confidently, as though it were the truth? Would you cave and believe what they tell you about your hair or eye color? The brain works in mysterious ways, and if you allow someone else to dictate your value, your innermost thoughts may go along with whatever they are saying about you. And what about those things that people say that are not visible? If you believe things that people say about you, or when you have a particular perception about yourself, your brain will look for evidence that it's true. Of course, your brain will find it.

Mindset Shift: I value myself.

This is where your true self versus your false self comes into play. When Emma heard that her hair was disgusting, she ultimately believed the person who told her this because she trusted that adult. She grew up believing that her true self had disgusting hair. It wasn't until she met her roommate, Shayna--who kept calling Emma's hair "gorgeous"--that Emma started to have a different perception of her hair. For the first time, Emma asked herself aloud, "How does my hair play a role in how I feel about myself? How do I begin to feel better about myself and stop buying into what was said to me in the past--and what I keep repeating to myself about myself in the present?"

*   *   *

Emma had finished her latte. She was looking at me.

"Remember when I encouraged you to get clear on your own qualities?" I said.

"The emotional connection to my positive thoughts helps instill new thinking and beliefs about myself," she said proudly. Then she repeated the question, as though pondering it for herself instead of asking me. "How does my hair play a role in how I feel about myself?"

I looked at her hair. It was lovely.

Abruptly, she made a statement. "There seems to be more to this Mastering Resilience process than replacing negative thoughts with positive ones."

*   *   *

Now, you may be asking, "Lorry, how the heck do I simply just turn my negative emotions into positive ones? That doesn't sound very easy!" It's not. But it's simple. I've compiled all the crucial steps necessary to change your negative thought patterns once and for all and to take more action being the best version of yourself. I call it the AAAs of Mastering Resilience:

Be **A**ware.

Acknowledge the Truth.

Take **A**ction.

> *Knowledge is power, and it can help you overcome any fear of the unexpected. When you learn, you gain more awareness through the process, and you know what pitfalls to look for as you get ready to transition to the next level.*
>
> —*Jay Shetty*

The first *A* of the AAAs of Mastering Resilience, Be **A**ware means: be present in the moment and be aware of your overall experience. Be aware of what you're telling yourself, be aware of your physical body; in other words, be aware of your thoughts, feelings, posture, and surroundings.

The definition of "aware" is "having knowledge of a situation or fact." If you're constantly telling yourself negative things about yourself, it becomes who you think you are. You only have knowledge of negative stories.

If you're telling yourself, "I'm so stupid," or "I keep making the same mistakes over and over again," be aware of the language your inner critic (or your false sense of self) is telling you. Notice how you are feeling and where those feelings manifest in your body. Do you get tightness in your throat? Do you constantly have a headache? How does your heart feel? Do you feel constriction in your chest? Are you hunched? Is your posture closed? Is your head down? Are your shoulders scrunched?

Be aware of your feelings and how they negatively or positively affect your body. Bring them to consciousness, take hold of those thoughts, and dismiss them with the evidence of your true self—your intrinsic value.

> *The strongest force in the universe is a human being living consistently with his identity.*
>
> —*Tony Robbins*

In the second *A* of the AAAs of Mastering Resilience, you get to **Acknowledge** the Truth about yourself. You get to acknowledge your intrinsic value. And you can physically change your posture to be consistent with the words, "I am confident." By acknowledging your true self, you will ultimately counteract your false sense of self. The definition of "acknowledge" is "to accept or admit the existence or truth of."

Take a key step by shifting your posture. Social psychologist Dr. Amy Cuddy argues that body language impacts how others see us, and that it also affects how we see ourselves. Just by sitting upright, you can shift your feelings. Sit up, roll your shoulders back, and hold your head up. Move your body in ways that demonstrate your truth.

Then, recite your "I am" statements from the previous chapter. If you haven't created them yet, say the following Mindset Shifts aloud with me:

1. I am worthy, I am enough.

2. I am here for a purpose.

3. I am a loyal and loving _____. (Fill in the blank: spouse, friend, etc.)

4. I am a great _____. (parent, sibling, coworker, etc.)

5. My purpose is _____. (I.e., to be a vessel of love designed to help heal the brokenhearted, etc.)

6. I am a compassionate person who sees the good in people.

7. I am brilliant.

8. I am a bright light that ignites the spark in people that fuels their confidence.

9. I am a healer.

10. I am a warrior.

11. I am resilient.

Let yourself feel the power of the words. Express these words profoundly within your consciousness and simultaneously tell your unconscious the truth. Acknowledge that *this* is your true self. Reframe the negative thoughts.

(I feel broken).

I am exactly where I'm supposed to be on this journey.

(I feel disgusting).

I am valuable.

(I was told I am a horrible, stupid idiot).

I am pure love.

To experience the value of the AAAs, it's crucial to understand clarity of self, as described in the last chapter, and the connection between what we tell ourselves about ourselves and why that's so important. As you meditate on this concept, play a song that resonates with you if you want to. One of my ultimate favorite songs is "The Champion" by Carrie Underwood featuring Ludacris. I also love "Rise" by Katy Perry, and "Girl on Fire" by Alicia Keys.

Action is the antidote to despair.

—Joan Baez

The third *A* in the AAAs of Mastering Resilience is to take **A**ction. But all action isn't created equally. "Action" may mean "the accomplishment of a thing, usually over a period of time, in stages, or with the possibility of repetition," but the action we're talking about here is action consistent with your truth and borne of self-love; it's action in keeping with and/or moving in the direction of your overall BIG Why.

Remembering and acknowledging your BIG Why, as well as your Why NOW commitment as the motivating forces for this healing journey, keep us going. Everybody can make choices to be successful and take specific action in the direction of their dreams and goals. You have the power to be successful on your own terms. The little choices and actions you take every day ultimately make a difference. You don't have to suddenly stop all behaviors that no longer serve you. That's not realistic, and if you were able to do it in the short run, it's not sustainable over a long period of time.

Create Action toward your BIG Why. Celebrate the progress, especially the wins.

*   *   *

The AAAs of Mastering Resilience can be used as often as necessary to get back on track if you find yourself ruminating on negative thoughts. Once you become Aware of thoughts that don't serve you, Acknowledge your "I am" statements (feeling the positive energy of the power of your true value), you can take Action consistent with your true identity in the direction of your BIG Why. Then celebrate the progress. On this journey, remember to pay attention to your thoughts and *be aware, acknowledge your true self,* and *take decisive action* towards your dreams and goals. At the end of the day, reflect on your BIG Why once again. It's so freeing to be able to shift from a negative perspective to a positive one in such a simple way.

Part of my own healing journey has been incorporating questions like, "Which thoughts are real? Which thoughts tell me more about who I truly am as a person?" It's imperative to understand how the false self, or *imposter syndrome*, comes into play in our lives. Though the behaviors I exhibited in my past may seem dysfunctional, I now understand they were normal reactions to abnormal circumstances.

You may have experienced shame from past choices too. You may have experienced adversities like me, and you may be wondering how you can learn more about your true self and apply the AAAs of Mastering Resilience. I can promise you that there is hope. Your coping mechanism may vary. You may have poured yourself into work, food, medication, social media, or something else to drown out your inner critic.

The result of this behavior, unfortunately, is believing that your false self is your true self––but this idea couldn't be further from the truth. I've met so many people at conferences, retreats, exhibitions, and more throughout the years who have similar backgrounds to mine. Some were teachers. Many had advanced degrees. Successful businesses. Six-figure incomes. Yet, they thought they were frauds. They truly believed in their false sense of identity and believed they were imposters––as did I.

I learned I had the ability to choose differently. I needed to understand how I was making my life choices. My behaviors were often consistent with the negative things that I told myself about myself. I named my inner critic, or my false self, "Scaredy Cat," because the motivation was fear. If it helps, you can nickname your inner critic too. I realized that "Scaredy Cat" wanted to run the show of my life. She wanted to be in charge. But my true self became louder and louder, as I added the AAAs of Mastering Resilience into my own day-to-day habits.

Our positive qualities, achievements, and personality traits are elements of our true identities. We all have individual superpowers. It's just a matter of finding out what our superpowers are and then choosing to use these superpowers effectively in our choices.

Not only did I name my inner critic, but I also named my successful self my superhero self. I encourage you to do the same. Acknowledge yourself by identifying and naming your inner superhero. I chose Wonder Woman because she was the only female superhero I was familiar with growing up. After doing more research, I found out that Wonder Woman's motivation always comes from love. There's no fear in love.

There are many ways to acknowledge your true self if you have trouble creating a list of "I am" statements. Long ago, I created a gratitude journal on one side of a notebook. It wasn't a fancy notebook; it had a plain turquoise cover with wide-ruled pages inside. Every morning, I began writing down three gratitude statements. I started allowing myself to be in a state of gratitude from the moment I woke up in the morning. This was difficult for me at first, but I learned that the simplest things could be written down—like having a warm cup of coffee in my favorite mug; enjoying my favorite food; having a warm bed to sleep in every night.

In the same notebook, I started a celebration journal from the back end, where I acknowledged and allowed myself to celebrate all sorts of accomplishments. I had gotten this idea from a friend, who explained to me that celebrating our wins daily can change the way our brain behaves and the way we go about our daily lives. Some examples included celebrating when I completed my To Do list for the day, accomplished a personal best at the gym, or when a big project was completed. I learned to celebrate the small wins along with the big ones.

Whenever I became aware of a negative thought that arose throughout the day, I was able remind myself what I was grateful for as well as what I was celebrating. I allowed myself to acknowledge the negative thought, but rather than acting on that one meager thought, I acted on my positive thoughts instead. These positive thoughts ranged from, "Lorry, you've been in tough situations before, and I know you can get through this" to "Lorry, think about the wonderful life you have with yourself and your family. You are unstoppable!"

Knowing yourself, your preferences, and your tendencies ultimately allows you to form a clear picture of the person you are and the person you want to become. To clarify who you are, you must first believe in your intrinsic value and the part you play in the world. Even if you were told your hair was disgusting, like Emma was, you get to question this belief. Once you do so, you might recognize that this belief came from someone else--**and**

you made it your own. Even if you made self-destructive choices in the past, like I did, you can begin the process of forgiving yourself and moving forward. These beliefs became a part of your false self. These past beliefs do not define your intrinsic value. Knowing your own intrinsic value is the foundation of your identity. This feeds into your true self.

*   *   *

Though I worked hard in school, I was still making self-destructive choices. My false self, or my inner critic's voice, was louder than my true self. I told myself, "You don't deserve to be alive. Nobody wants you here. You're a piece of shit." And I believed those voices, despite my efforts to live a life in which I would help others. I carried so much shame about my past choices, and I punished myself in accordance with who I believed I was. I believed my true self included making these poor, self-destructive decisions. The person my professor saw was simply a fake. A phony.

I used to refer to myself as "irreparably broken," even after years of therapy, reading mounds of self-help books, and spending thousands of dollars on personal development programs.

I used to believe the adversity I experienced defined me and defined my capabilities as a human being.

**Mindset Shift: I am in control of the choices I make
in my own life.**

What you say to yourself about yourself becomes a part of your identity. Yet mistakes are opportunities for learning as are successes. I chose to learn from my mistakes. The value I placed on my future and my own choices held greater value to me than mistakes from my past. We can choose to believe we are children of God, worthy and highly favored, or you can define your value in ways that are meaningful to you. I use the AAAs to imbed the truth about who I am into my day-to-day experiences and choices.

You may have experienced shame from past choices as well. You may have experienced adversities and you may be wondering how you can learn more about your true self. I promise you again that there is hope.

Someone once said to me, "Stand in front of the mirror and say, 'I am worthy,' until you believe it." I felt I could've been standing there for decades, staring at myself, seeing everything that was wrong with me. If you want to try to stand in front of the mirror and say empowering words to yourself, you should. Not every piece of advice is going to help you along your healing journey, and it's okay to acknowledge that too.

For me, standing in front of the mirror didn't help. I didn't feel any positive shift in my thinking. Now I know words alone don't make mindset shifts. The words must be accompanied by practicing empathy towards ourselves, conjuring and imagining what it FEELS like to be worthy, to shift the mindset. That's what the AAAs of Mastering Resilience do. It's the ingredient that makes the recipe work. It's like the baking powder that gets sprinkled in to activate the recipe and allows the cake to rise.

As the ingredients get blended together, though, we sometimes forget to warm up the oven. This applies to Mastering Resilience, as well.

One of my goals over the past couple of years was to be committed to my physical health. I started an exercise regimen to keep my body strong. I can show up right on time for the workout. I can work with the trainer and get some benefits from the exercise. I might feel stronger and notice my body changing.

However, if I get to the gym a few minutes early, I have time to prepare my body. I might take the foam roller and roll out some kinks in my muscles. I may do some movements to warm up my body. I may get on the stationary bike and pedal slowly to loosen my muscles.

Consider this "warm up" as your new morning routine—waking up and imagining your BIG Why, reading your BIG Why, and allowing yourself to experience the emotions of achieving your dreams. The process of Mastering Resilience is most effective when you read your BIG Why every single day. You refer to your Why NOW as a means of staying connected to your current choices in life. You'll be prepared for the day, much like being prepared for a workout. Joints loosen, heart rate's a little boosted, and you have a greater range of motion because the muscles were rolled out. There's more benefit because everything is warmed up.

The time you spend reflecting on your BIG Why, your Healing Pledge, and your "I am" mindset shift statements are all intended to keep you warmed up to get the full benefit of the other healing applications. This time lays the groundwork for being intentional throughout the day for opportunities to use the AAAs of Mastering Resilience. Several people who have used this recipe set a timer throughout the day and check in with themselves. Some use the ingredient when they realize they were triggered at some point during the day. Either way, it works to make it part of the daily routine.

In my workout routine, I also take the time to stretch my muscles afterward. When I stretch, I don't get so sore after the workout, and I'm more likely to be back in the gym the next day. The stretching is the self-care afterwards—the celebration and acknowledgement of a job well done. It's the thing that helps the muscles recover from the exertion of exercise.

On this journey, remember to read your Healing Pledge and to pay attention to your thoughts. Stretch yourself throughout the day by being aware, acknowledging your true self, and taking decisive action towards your dreams and goals.

Mindset Shift: I am willing to try different methods to achieve my goals while acknowledging that every mechanism will not necessarily work well for me as an individual.

CHAPTER SIX

Compassion
for Self and Others

*When we give ourselves compassion, we are opening
our hearts in a way that can transform our lives.*

--Kristin Neff

There is growing evidence that self-compassion may be one of
our top defenses--and that defense develops in childhood.
In a 2020 study published in *Mindfulness*, researchers reported
"With rates of bias-based bullying, general peer victimization,
sex assigned at birth, and ACEs held constant, all identity groups
experienced lower rates of mental health concerns when they
reported higher self-compassion" (Vigna et al.). To help youth
practice self-compassion, we must work on practicing compassion ourselves.

*   *   *

Over morning coffee, Emma and I started discussing the idea of
compassion.

"Lorry, I don't know about you, but all of this work I'm doing on myself...well, I guess I'm starting to learn more about not only myself, but also about my parents."

Emma had a very good therapist that she was seeing weekly. She'd sometimes revisit the issues she discussed in those sessions, like we sometimes do with friends.

"I felt so angry toward my dad for leaving us," Emma said, "even though it was more than twenty years ago. I carried that anger with me and felt it within my heart for years. But lately, I'm feeling something new, something unfamiliar..."

I had a gut feeling. "Could it be compassion?" I'd gone through this same journey with my mom.

"YES!" Pulling out her phone, she read the definition of "compassion" aloud. "'Sympathetic consciousness of others' distress together with a desire to alleviate it.'"

I nodded.

"It's almost like I can forgive my dad, and myself, finally." Tears started to well up in her eyes. She said they were happy tears. "I never thought I could do that. When he left and when we ended up moving from place to place, I blamed him. I blamed him and his leaving for all my bad choices, all the mistakes, all the bad boyfriends, all the anger I felt, pushing others away from me for so many years...but I can see now that this is a long process to learn and grow on my own terms."

The warm smile that came across my face was so genuine. I was so happy for her.

"Emma, part of having compassion for others and for ourselves is also learning how to be vulnerable. It's understanding that we're able to move toward forgiveness in a way that serves us and shows compassion for them. And it also means having compassion for ourselves, for our past mistakes. Forgiveness feels like such a big lift, sometimes of biblical proportions, but compassion?, that's more manageable, more doable." I took a deep breath. "Remember, this is a journey I've taken too."

*   *   *

When we're growing up, we frequently hear statements about our intrinsic value and who we are, even as young children. You may've heard positive affirmations, like, "Great job!" or "I'm so proud of you!" when you scored a goal on the soccer field, or when you helped clean up dishes. You may've heard negative comments, like, "I can't believe you were born; you were an accident; you're worthless," very similar to things I heard. This verbiage sticks with us through adulthood, and what we hear as children can become the ultimate definition we have of ourselves. If you only hear negative comments growing up, then that's what your adult self may have internalized as real. Compassion for self and others can be very healing and freeing.

I vividly remember my mother leaning against the kitchen wall while she talked to her friends. She'd always hold the yellow receiver of the dial telephone hanging on the matching kitchen wall. It was a common place for her to be when I came home from school. I remember overhearing my mom say that she wished I'd never been born—as well as a slew of other things she said directly to me that stuck with me profoundly. When I was just sixteen years old, we were arguing in front of the stove when she shouted, "If I'd known what you were going to turn out like, I would've had an abortion."

I took this message to heart. For years, I believed the world would be better off without me. I judged myself—and I judged my mother.

As an adult, however, I came to understand her perspective and why she may have been triggered to say such hurtful words to her own daughter. Those words revealed more about her and her situation than they ever did about me.

Just a little over a year before this conversation in the kitchen, I'd revealed that my "dad" had sexually abused me. The fallout was immense. It seemed to me that that one revelation ended her marriage, her sense of financial security, and upended her entire world. Suddenly, she was a single mother of four—and she blamed me.

But the blaming had begun long before that. The affair my mom had during her first marriage when she was nineteen years old that her husband discovered–, that man she had an affair with, my biological father, the "love of her life," didn't stay with her; neither did her first husband. Surely, her own behavior in those relationships influenced their outcome.

But from my mom's perspective, I wrecked her life by being born.

During the conversation in her bedroom when I was twenty-two, she'd said, "Every time I look at you, I see his face...and I hate him for leaving." At that time, I didn't make the connection between her hatred toward my biological father and her hateful words and actions toward me. Only later would I come to realize the full extent of her trauma.

I was deeply hurt by her words. I internalized them and made them my own. I thought I didn't deserve to live. I was full of self-hatred. My behaviors were harmful and self-destructive. I used to think these words described the truth about my identity. The words that spat out of her mouth toward me made me not only feel terrible toward her, but also toward myself. After going through therapy, and rehashing that conversation hundreds of times in my head, —the mean, hateful words she said to me—I learned these words did not, and do not, define who I am.

Mindset Shift: The words uttered throughout my childhood by others do not define my true self.

"Forgive and forget" was a household dictum when I was growing up. As a child, I wondered, *How is anyone really supposed to do that?* Forgiveness is the conscious, deliberate decision to release feelings of resentment or vengeance toward a person or group who has harmed you. It's not forgetting; it's not denying the severity of the incident, and it's certainly not condoning or making excuses for them. No obligation comes with forgiveness, least of all the obligation to reconcile or relieve the person of accountability for their harmful behavior.

When I was younger, I knew my lack of forgiveness was hurting me. Being in a state of anger, feeling like a victim, and being stuck in the past were not serving me. It's important to acknowledge here that I consider my personal journey to be a spiritual one. I believe there is a God who is the creator of the Universe. After praying to God and thinking about my state of mind for some time, I landed on a definition of forgiveness that I could live with.

Treat them differently than they "deserve" to be treated.

It was a good first step. This allowed me to respond empathetically (an element of compassion), to behave with kindness and in accord with my own values, and to give grace in the face of mistakes--all unconditionally. I decided to have compassion for others while I was also practicing compassion for myself.

My definition acknowledged that the adults in my life inflicted harm, that it was wrong, and that though responding with anger felt appropriate, it wasn't a response that served my best and highest good. In retrospect, it meant I believed they deserved to be perpetually punished. Holding on to the anger and resentment hurt *me*. So, I began to treat people differently. With compassion.

I was not treating anyone differently with any expectation that I would receive anything in return. I was treating people indifferently, and eventually compassionately, also as an act of compassion for myself. It was an active, intentional choice to be compassionate rather than bitter or resentful, and it brought me peace of mind.

Suddenly, I could let go of all those deeply held negative feelings toward my mom and others who had said hateful words to me or hurt me in the past, which had become imbedded in my false sense of self. I began to tie compassion into my true self. Suddenly, I recognized the pain that had been inflicted without letting the pain define me. I began to heal and move on with my life.

Having compassion also means being able to make the distinction between "I am bad" and "I made a bad decision." Self-compassion is not the same as self-indulgence. It took me years to show myself the same kindness I eventually afforded those who'd wronged me in the past.

There is a significant relationship between compassion and resilience—the ability to skillfully cope with adversity. When we are self-compassionate, we treat ourselves tenderly, fairly, and warmly, with loving-kindness, no matter what circumstances we find ourselves in. And when we're dealing with adverse experiences, self-compassion goes a long way; it fuels resilience and coping, according to the team at the Resiliency Center at the University of Utah, furthering our well-being, especially in response to trauma and stress. "When we go through major life crises, self-compassion appears to make all the difference in our ability to survive and even thrive."

And yet, mistakes often inspire our worst self-treatment. Many of us ruminate for days over the smallest blunders and spiral into a state of paralysis, refusing to make a move in fear of another error. We operate on autopilot, devoid of emotions, and get by working on the minimum necessary. It's a miserable way to be.

Of course, mistakes are part of the learning process. When we learned to walk or ride a bike, we fell down a lot.

But for many of us, the standard we set for ourselves as adults is perfection. There is no room for mistakes. Over the years, many of my clients, supervisees, and mentees have shared experiences of beating themselves up for the mistakes and mishaps of the past. The result? Relentless self-sabotage and constant self-defeating patterns and behaviors. I'm here to tell you that there is freedom that comes with this simple mindset shift.

Mindset Shift: Perfection is not a realistic standard.

How often do we achieve a goal only to go on to the next milestone without a simple celebration or acknowledgement? It's so consistent with never feeling good enough, always striving for the next best thing. Yet, celebrating even the small wins is self-affirming. It's an honorable, compassionate thing to do. Once we've achieved a level of compassion for ourselves, it is so much easier to have compassion for others.

As we become masters of resilience, we begin to have compassion toward ourselves and toward others, including those who have wronged us in the past.

Compassion for ourselves is associated with well-being, better physical health, fewer injuries, and better self-regulation, as well as self-care. Compassion for others shows that you care. But, oddly enough, compassion sometimes gets a bad rap. Just a few of the myths I've heard about self-compassion include:

Myth No. One: Thinking of yourself first is conceited or selfish. If you cooked dinner, it's not polite to serve yourself first. Better let others serve themselves first so they don't go hungry.

Myth No. Two: Your worth comes from putting others first. People pleasing is a good thing, always.

Becoming resilient is the very thing that allows us to reframe our trauma adversity, including ACEs. By continuing to practice compassion towards ourselves, as well as loving-kindness towards others, we ultimately build our resilience. Compassion for self and others is the sweetener in the recipe for mastering resilience. It's like the sugar or honey (or sugar substitute) that makes the cake sweet and tasty.

In *What Happened To You?: Conversations on Trauma, Resilience, and Healing,* Dr. Bruce D. Perry and Oprah Winfrey share an extended dialogue that uses Winfrey's life, including her ACE-laden childhood, to reframe how we think about trauma and healing. In the book, Winfrey writes:

> When you've been groomed to be compliant, confrontation in any form is uncomfortable because you were never taught that you have the right to say 'no'; in fact, you were taught that you can't say 'no.' The sense that you aren't deserving enough to set your own boundaries has been stolen from you. Many people react by burying their feelings of 'no' and becoming people pleasers.

It's really important to never define yourself by acts of kindness that you perform for others alone. Acknowledge your true self, (you can go back to the chapter on Clarity of Self and explore your likes and dislikes, as well as how you view your own intrinsic value for a refresher). Once you establish this clarity, you can learn to undo your people-pleasing habits and tendencies. This doesn't mean you aren't kind, loving, or generous. If this is in accordance with your true self, then act that way. But if you find yourself only giving to others and not giving to yourself, ask yourself, "How can I act with more compassion towards myself while still maintaining my true identity?" Acts of compassion are kind, encouraging, motivating, nurturing, and helpful. Remember, this is applicable to how you treat yourself just as much as how you treat others.

People pleasing has long since been an accepted virtue in our culture. If you're a people pleaser, though, you may not be allowing your own needs to hold the same weight as those of others. Rather than focusing on putting yourself first, try putting yourself equal, at least initially. You might have to work to reframe assertive behaviors. Remember, putting yourself first does not make you selfish. Putting yourself first fuels you, so you have more to give.

Have you ever heard of the analogy, "Fill your own cup so you can pour it into others?" It's okay to consider the needs of others, though not at the expense of yourself. When we practice self-compassion with acceptance, we not only accept ourselves for who we are, but also accept that bad things can happen to us and within our world. We're not required to respond negatively with blame, shame, or punishment. We can choose how we respond to our experiences and how we respond to what we are given in life. We can respond with empathy, understanding, and compassion instead of anger, resentment, and victimization. I firmly believe that you are doing the best you can, given any circumstances that come your way.

Once we've achieved a level of compassion for ourselves, it is so much easier to have compassion for others. Compassion for ourselves allows us to have compassion for others. Holding onto resentment prevents us from progressing. Resentment is the opposite of compassion. I realized this the hard way, when I held on to so much resentment toward my mom for many years. My mother began to drink heavily after divorcing her third husband, when I was around fourteen years old. She said very hateful things when she was drunk. It was easy to tell myself a story of how much she hated me, or that she didn't want me, and wished I wasn't around. Much later in my life, when I was able to see her as a young child in an abusive, alcoholic home, I could see that the choices she made for herself and in her life came from her own woundedness. I told myself a different story about why she said the things she did, and the story wasn't about me. Hurt people hurt people. When we truly grasp that concept, it's easier to respond with compassion, both to others and to ourselves. Knowing that, I was able to forgive her, show compassion toward her, and take care of her while she was sick and dying. Viewing my mother with compassion didn't excuse her behavior, but it helped me a lot.

Mindset Shift: The way other people treat me doesn't need to change the story I tell myself about myself.

I didn't learn about the ACEs science until after my mom's passing. When I considered her circumstances in the light of that research, it led me to feel even greater compassion for her and the life she led. All the risk factors were there. Secrets riddled our family, and the specific circumstances of my mother's childhood are buried with her. She rarely discussed her own past. In retrospect, I know she carried deep and damaging shame throughout her life.

When I considered her circumstances in the context of ACEs science, not only did I forgive my mom completely, but I also recommitted my life's work to helping others realize the ravaging impact of Adverse Childhood Experiences when there is little or no intervention. I do this by knowing, sharing, and training others about the original ACE study, as well as the toxic stress response to ACEs and other related life events. Part of my mission is helping people understand the context of their circumstances and behavior.

Compassion for others may prompt forgiveness, though forgiveness isn't mandatory. In *Psychology Today*, trauma psychotherapist Amanda Ann Gregory suggests that expecting those who have experienced trauma to forgive may be harmful, especially if it requires a person to confront an abuser or if the act of forgiveness keeps them in harm's way. Forgiving, according to Gregory, perpetuates the violence of the trauma.

Acts of compassion, on the other hand, do not require this of you. Compassion is an internal process that ultimately changes how we see another person. When we empathize with people who have hurt us, and realize that they may be hurting, too, we can see the situation from the other person's perspective and move toward feelings of compassion.

Everyone collects scabs and scars, visible and invisible, along their healing journey. You are not alone in feeling the burden of the weight of unforgiveness and resentment.

But that weight can be lifted. That pain can be alleviated. The motivation of the people who hurt us, the potential reasons for their behavior, were never about us. We often blame ourselves for the actions of others, thinking our actions inspired the hurt, like I did as a teenager. I figured I was wrong for being born. The pain my mother's words inflicted upon me was a reflection of her own pain. It's easier to blame ourselves than confront someone else, especially if we don't have a sense of our boundaries or if we don't have the stamina to enforce our boundaries. Holding on to a story can be our way of holding on to our own ill-perceived truth about what happened.

We can also hang on to bruised feelings and hold grudges to convince ourselves that the situation wasn't our fault, especially in cases where the other person doesn't hold themselves accountable or accept responsibility for their actions. The explanation, not the excuse, was that the person who caused the pain was not accountable, so we may think we need to enforce culpability. Holding on to memories can be a way of holding them responsible--one that shields us from perceiving that it's "all our fault." Holding on to memories may serve to solidify holding on to shame and feelings of unworthiness from the past. The truth is, we all have our own version of a story that is true for us based on our own perception at the moment it took place. We can allow the story to be reframed in our own minds when we hear another version of the story. It doesn't mean we have to have a relationship with them to express compassion; it can be your own internal process.

When we respond with compassion, we're driven to make the world a better place. That's why so many resilient individuals who have experienced childhood adversity are often driven toward helping professions and positions: teaching, counseling, youth ministry, coaching, and mentoring. Our ability to be resilient in the face of adversity has a purpose.

Mindset Shift: I can be compassionate towards others, no matter the circumstances.

We can learn from our mistakes. We start to understand why we might not be able to achieve our next goal. In *What Happened To You?*, Winfrey and Perry consider patterns of stress activation. They illustrate how, if a child receives predictable, moderate, and controllable stress activators in their life, that child will have tolerance, or resilience, for what life has to offer. If a child receives unpredictable, extreme, or prolonged stress activators, then that child will experience sensitization and become vulnerable; "a cascade of risk in emotional, social, mental, and physical health occurs."

Allowing space for your emotions is also an act of self-compassion. Suppressing your emotions can cause physical issues within the body as well. When your stress levels are high, this can constrict your muscles and nerves, causing you to suffer from physical pain. Think about a time your emotions were at an all-time high. Was there physical pain in tandem? A migraine trigger, for instance, can be stress-induced. Sciatica pain might be a result of stress. Neck pain can also be a direct result of experiencing high-stress levels. When you experience physical discomfort, your nervous system is passing a signal to your brain that these emotions need to be understood and handled to reduce bodily tension you're experiencing. In fact, research shows that your gut has the same amount of serotonin as your brain. You can easily allow your negative emotions to cause you to spiral out of control down a rabbit hole. When your feelings do come out, they tend to be out of proportion and get released, often in unhealthy ways. This is why you may feel the urge to numb your negative emotions. Options to use instead of numbing strategies include the following:

Exercise: By releasing endorphins, you reduce feelings of negativity or anxiety. The mental health benefits of exercise are widely acknowledged. A 2020 study published in *Scientific Reports* found that strength training reduces symptoms of anxiety. Frequency of yoga practice was positively associated with levels of psychological wellbeing in a 2021 study published in *Journal of Family Medicine and Primary Care.* And the benefits go beyond bench pressing or downward dogs. Exercise at large, according to researchers in *The Journal of Clinical Psychiatry,* may "alleviate symptoms such as low self-esteem and social withdrawal."

Talking aloud: Talking about your feelings is a sign of strength. Sometimes talking things out with a friend or therapist helps you not only achieve your goals, but also to learn about your true self and your intrinsic value.

Writing: When you write, you can fully express yourself in ways you might not otherwise. Your thoughts and feelings have great value––and sometimes, an even greater meaning––when you write them down and are honest with yourself. You can give more meaning to how a traumatic experience, like ACEs, affected you, how you are committed to understanding what happened, and committed to learning more about your true self.

Think about a time when you told yourself you "don't deserve" that treat, that vacation, or even that walk outside. By continuing to tell yourself that you "don't deserve" that, you are ultimately creating a barrier between your true self and your ability to have compassion for yourself. Having compassion facilitates authenticity, boundaries, and lower levels of emotional turmoil in your life.

An important note: one of the *greatest acts of self-compassion is setting boundaries. Setting boundaries is an act of self-love.* There's a fine line between being a good friend or Samaritan and having boundaries. If a friend calls at midnight and needs your help with her child because her husband suddenly fell ill, you would go help in a heartbeat; that's who you are. But if a friend calls you every single day asking for help and you put off sleep, work, or any self-care activity to help this friend, you may have a boundary problem. When you have good boundaries in your life, you can achieve your accomplishments or even allow space to properly take care of yourself. Good, solid, and safe boundaries are practiced with compassion and forgiveness.

Mindset Shift: My mistakes are part of the learning process in my healing journey.

I urge you to start speaking to yourself with more compassion. What would you say to someone else who experienced similar adversities to you? Ask yourself if you have compassion for that person's inner child, and if you're able to have compassion for your own inner child too. How would you shift what you're telling yourself?

CHAPTER SEVEN

The BOTH™ Approach: The Secret Sauce of Mastering Resilience

A journey of a thousand miles begins with a single step.

—Lao Tzu

In a 2014 study by researchers at San Francisco State University, guided cognitive reframing helped adolescents understand conflict with stepfathers. According to Cookston et al., "More frequent reframing was associated with more adaptive cognitive explanations for father/stepfather behavior." Cognitive reframing has the power to help us make sense of complicated, discordant, or difficult situations. We owe it to ourselves, and the children we serve, to act.

*   *   *

Home was never a safe place for Alex. Growing up, he witnessed atrocious behavior, domestic violence of all sorts. Alex described that his father would brutally punch his mother in a drunken rage while he and his siblings watched from the staircase. His mother would yell at the children in the house when they engaged in ordinary childlike behaviors, kid stuff, like spilling water or laughing or acting silly—these yells would identify anything that could provoke Alex's father's rage. He and his siblings were young, just seven, six, and five, when they entered the foster care system.

Alex and his siblings learned it wasn't safe to be themselves. They couldn't laugh at a joke, eat messy foods, or be playful for fear of being abused.

Alex learned to self-soothe by grinding his teeth. As an adult, he was able to see an orthodontist and get braces to correct his teeth. But growing up, he didn't ever have that option. Alex also self-soothed by biting his nails, a common, unhealthy habit children may develop out of necessity. Alex felt these habits helped him feel alive when he was younger.

When home is not a safe place, children need ways to self-soothe to lower their anxiety, whether they are healthy or unhealthy methods of doing so. Soothing or engaging in numbing behaviors are perfectly normal reactions in the face of these adverse circumstances. During our weekly meetings, Alex and I further discussed his tumultuous childhood. Though we didn't talk about ACEs at the time, we certainly spoke about trauma and how it continued to play a role in his life today.

"I sometimes bite my nails...I still grind my teeth," sighed Alex. "On the days I have a full caseload and I see clients facing circumstances similar to my own childhood...well, those are the days I find myself biting my nails more often and seem to have a grinding issue at night."

"You're aware that you're doing these things, though," I said. "Maybe it's worth taking your healing to the next level.

Alex put down his black pen and notepad, and his left leg started to shake.

When I contemplate taking a case that is reminiscent of my own childhood, I understand that it's critically important to be aligned with my higher self, the best version of myself. I get to become aware of what my inner child is experiencing and acknowledge her—and my past—in the context of who I am today. I get to examine the meaning that I've placed on my past adversities, and how they've shaped who I have become. I get to examine whether my perspective will interfere with the treatment process with my clients. Then I know whether I can provide quality care for a particular client or whether I choose to consult with my own "supervisor" to ensure that I'm remaining objective and effective.

"You have an opportunity," I explained, to Alex, "to reframe the past if you're ready. Living through your adversities has ultimately empowered you to become the person you are, with the unique qualities that are making you the good therapist that you are today. It served to strengthen qualities that were already there in the first place. Also, living through these adversities may have masked or hidden other qualities that you get to uncover as you continue along this healing journey. Understanding the context of why you were grinding your teeth and biting your nails as a child is important. Bad things happened and you're right in perceiving they kept you alive at the time. Also, good things can come out of those bad things that happened."

Alex smiled and wrote something down on his notepad. I was happy to see he took some notes from our conversation. Alex always processed what he learned in supervision and used it to hone his skills as a therapist.

"Thank you, Lorry," he said. "This is truly mind-blowing. I'm learning so much from you, and I'm so glad I can continue my own healing journey while I'm learning how to be the best therapist I can be."

*   *   *

Since becoming a practicing psychologist many years ago, I've seen how focusing exclusively on the bad things that happened can be a source of unhappiness. I used to refer to myself as being irreparably broken. That's what inspired me to come with my own ingredient, the secret sauce of this amazing mastering resilience cake we are baking. The secret sauce has the combination of ingredients that make the cake unique and special, like the carrots and cream cheese of the carrot cake or the chocolate and coconut of a German chocolate cake. I call our next healing ingredient, The Bold Opportunity to Heal (The BOTH™ Approach).

The adverse experiences can result in numerous different and often conflicting feelings simultaneously––feelings that can be hard to navigate when they assault our bodies, minds, hearts, and souls. The BOTH Approach is a simple process that involves cognitive reframing and more.   This approach acknowledges that past adversities have BOTH good and bad (or not-so-good) qualities. Acknowledging that (when you're ready) allows you to approach the adversity from both perspectives to heal and move on.

You can be sad about the horrible things you witnessed, what was said to you in a negative context, or if you experienced abuse of any sort. You can feel a host of different emotions about your past. And also, you can also choose to concentrate on being pleased that you are who you are as a direct result of the adversities you experienced.

In the past, professionals in my field have recommended the following traditional methods of healing:

Rehash negative things that happened in the past;

Confront those who hurt you;

Being told to "forgive and forget";

Advice to leave the past behind and focus on the future;

Grieve the childhood you never had.

There are other remedies that can be helpful, of course, including prescriptions for self-care, exercise, and paying attention to your nutrition.

Yet, in my experience, the BOTH Approach significantly shortens the process by acknowledging the past for what it was while seeing, from a new perspective, how an adverse situation can have had a positive effect on your future.

The BOTH Approach does not tell you to constantly rehash the negativity you experienced.

The BOTH Approach does not tell you to "forgive and forget" or leave the past behind.

The BOTH Approach does not tell you to grieve the childhood you never had without looking at the full picture.

Ultimately, we assign meaning and purpose to every experience we've had. We are stronger individually because of these adversities. Living fully in the strength of our identity means focusing on the good. Staying in the past in the form of regret, revenge, victimhood, fear, and responding in those ways makes us miss out on opportunities to step into greatness and harness our superpowers.

You can already see the good—that's why you're here, reading this book, and wanting to become a helper and cycle breaker in this world. Maybe you've been a teacher for twenty years. Maybe you're about to become a social worker, or a psychologist and talk with people about their own healing journeys too. Perhaps you're a parent or an entrepreneur who wants to be successful in your own right.

You've already seen success in some form in your life. You may not be in love with every aspect of your life--or love many of the old habits you have--but when you look at yourself in the mirror, you know there is good in you and good surrounding you. The good that came out of adversity is your resilience, your compassion, your patience, and your forgiveness. Your goodness can turn into greatness.

Right now, I'm giving you a unique opportunity. You have a Bold Opportunity to Heal from your past circumstances. Instead of only feeling anger or resentment, for example, ask yourself, "What are the positive qualities of who I am today *because* of my adverse experiences?"

You are valuable. And intrinsically worthy. You are meant for greatness, regardless of what you've experienced.

Now we get to look at the "how" of your past. How did you experience these things in your past, and how did it affect you? Can you shift your perspective to see BOTH sides of the story— positive and negative?

Kintsugi, meaning golden ("*kin*") and repair ("*tsugi*"), is a traditional Japanese art form where cracked pottery is repaired with liquid gold. Kintsugi is widely known as a symbol of who we become in the face of trauma. Using a precious metal—gold, or other times silver or lacquer dusted with powdered gold—to bring together pieces of a broken vase or bowl both makes the object whole and, at the same time, enhances the breaks. The breakage may symbolize our perceived brokenness and the gold represents our strength and healing. This pottery can serve as a symbol that you are more valuable because adversity has strengthened you in your time of vulnerability, and healing has taken place.

You can choose to see yourself as beautiful as a kintsugi bowl—you can look at the gold as the greater value you have in the face of adversity. It's your compassion, patience, and understanding. It's your work ethic, your perseverance, your resilience, your loving-kindness...all the positive qualities that result from the adversity you experienced. The gold permeates the pottery, representing brokenness *and* beauty.

This is your inherent goodness, it's all of you.

I've acknowledged that healing ourselves is a moral obligation because our character impacts those around us and has a ripple effect in the world. We're automatically set apart from others with the adversities we've experienced, yet it's important to recognize that we can continue this healing process. You too can master the art of resilience, becoming a role model for others.

**Mindset Shift: The whole sum of my circumstances
has made me who I am today.**

There comes a time where you get to make a choice. You can choose to acknowledge the past you had, and you can choose to believe that some of your behaviors are based upon normal reactions to an abnormal set of circumstances, which is reassuring. Alternatively, you can choose to rehash the past, be dismissive about current negative behaviors, and not address the past in a healthy way.

I encourage you to make the first choice. Know that your current behaviors may no longer be serving you in good ways, and that it's not in line with the best version of yourself. Your intrinsic value is important to acknowledge as well. We are transforming our adversity into our purpose. We are the helpers, breaking the cycle for the next generation to become who they are meant to be.

*   *   *

I've come across many people in the psychology field who are in the process of taking their exams, including Alex. Even though they may feel confident while preparing for these licensing exams, they may fail, like I did.

It was at that weird transition moment when my formal education life was ending and my professional life was beginning. I had finished my classes; I'd acquired my master's degree and my Ph.D. I was left with the set clinical hours to be licensed as a psychologist. At that time, you could begin work as a registered psychologist with a supervisor, which is what I did.

Back then, to become a licensed psychologist, you had to take both written and oral psychology licensing exams. These exams were only offered twice a year.

The first time I took the written licensing exam, I failed. I waited the few weeks it took after taking the exam and anxiously checked my mailbox, in anticipation of receiving the packet from the licensing board. When I slipped the key into the mailbox and slid open the door, I saw the letter-sized envelope with the return address from the licensing board. I knew immediately that I hadn't passed. A passing result came in a manila envelope with all the requisite paperwork to sign up for the oral exam. I was standing in the courtyard of my apartment building, and I stomped my foot and screamed. I'm not sure if the words came out of my mouth, or if they remained in my head. *This does NOT happen to me! I graduated from UCLA! I taught college and graduate level psychology for four flippin' years!* I raged inside for days before finally accepting that I'd failed. But I didn't stop at acknowledging that I failed the exam. I spiraled. I wasn't just an exam failure; I was a failure as a person. All I saw were flaws in and outside of myself. I berated myself, asking how I could possibly fail such a huge exam. This was my career, for crying out loud! I'd worked so hard to get where I was. I didn't, at least at first, ask myself how there could be anything positive surrounding this circumstance.

The second time around—six months later—I passed the written exam. I'd reached the conclusion that I didn't have enough respect for the examination process. I thought that since I'd taught so many undergraduate courses in psychology and graduate level courses, including psychopathology, I knew the content inside and out. But I hadn't prepared to take *this* test. I studied differently the second time around. I went to the library and simulated the several hours-long test, every week for twelve weeks until I repeatedly obtained a passing score on the practice exams.

I shifted to studying for the orals and took them a few weeks later. The oral exams were always conducted in a hotel. All the aspiring psychologists lined up in a long hallway waiting for their names to be called. Once called, we followed two examiners into a hotel room for the exam. The oral exams were clinical vignettes with case examples very similar to the cases I was accustomed to treating in the community mental health setting. I was anxious, more than I thought I would be, and second-guessed myself. I asked if I could change my answer and then I proceeded to. The two examiners looked at each other, and though they were trained to be stoic during the exam, I sensed I failed it then and there. I was right. The envelope was once again letter sized. I was devastated. The process to get licensed could have taken a few weeks, but in my case, extended to nearly a year and a half, more than triple the amount of time.

Later, I realized I had to heal from this adversity as much as if it had occurred during childhood and in much the same way. Instead of seeing only the negative side of what happened to me, I started to tell myself that this was simply a part of my journey, and there was a good reason this happened, even if I didn't yet know what it was. Acknowledging that this was a difficult experience was extraordinarily important. Yet being able to come to a place where I could acknowledge the good parts of this experience was important too.

When Alex approached me after he found out about his licensing exam, he was in tears.

"Lorry, I felt so confident going into my exams," he wept. "I feel horrible about myself, and now I'm questioning my BIG Why. Should I even be a therapist? Does that even make sense?"

He dropped his files down on the floor in my office and covered his face with his hands.

I sat there quietly for a moment and let him collect himself. Then, I spoke, wanting to tell him my exam story, hoping it would bring him hope.

"Alex, did you know that I failed my licensing exam too?"

He looked at me. Then his posture changed dramatically. The tears stopped. "YOU?"

"I failed the written and the orals," I said.

"Well, if you failed, then I don't feel so bad." He laughed.

"You'll pass," I said very confidently.

Here it was, the good that came out of failing my exams. Now Alex had hope.

During your healing process, it's important to acknowledge any hurt you felt while also being mindful and intentional about anything worthwhile that has come from your past. This is different from so-called "toxic positivity," or the belief that no matter how bad a situation is, you should remain positive. We get to acknowledge that bad things happen--that they were bad, unfortunate, awful, hurtful, and even wrong--while also recognizing the precious value that gives meaning to that adversity. Because adversity *does* produce positive outcomes. Your very survival is a testament to that. The "I am" statements you practiced earlier are often the byproducts of the challenges you've experienced. It will allow your positive qualities to emerge and further develop and anchor in your "I am" statements, to develop even deeper and further into how you perceive yourself and recognize and acknowledge your true self, with intrinsic value and all the attributes that allow you to have such a positive and lasting impact on those around you.

CHAPTER EIGHT

Cognitive Reframing:
Your Personal BOTH™ Approach

Planning an event, focusing on work, juggling competing tasks, remembering to pick up the dry cleaning—executive function is crucial to nearly all aspects of our lives. Yet for youth with ACEs or trauma, executive function is often disrupted. The long-term effects of compromised executive function could be calamitous for youth––even more reason for us to step up.

*   *   *

During the 2008 financial crisis, everything in my life that could go wrong did. Or so it seemed. In planning to alternatives for future retirement, Gary and I had invested in real estate. We bought our first property in 2003 and our last at the end of 2006, which happened to be the peak of the real estate market at the time. Shortly afterwards, the market tanked. We saw the writing on the wall, but surely we had enough in our reserves to ride out the storm…right?

A series of unfortunate events occurred, one after another. Heaters in the rental units went out in the winter. Air conditioners went out in the summer. A sewer flooded a first-floor unit. Tenants started to lose their jobs. They couldn't make rent, yet we couldn't bring ourselves to evict them. By the end of 2008, our reserves were depleted. The media conglomerates were vilifying real estate investors like us; they were saying, "They're greedy, they did this to themselves…it serves them right." From our perspective at the time, we used conventional wisdom, and we sought what we believed was wise counsel. We had no idea the market would crash in the way it did. I felt like I was failing as a wife, a mother, a friend, a boss, and a worker. I even felt like I was failing spiritually, especially when I heard the news commentary decry investors' greed and barrage them with blame for this systemic mess. And it wasn't just the news. Acquaintances who found out about our situation would say things like, "Lorry, it's your fault, you signed the loan papers." Translation (to my brain), "Yes, I'm a complete and utter failure." There it was, that familiar, horrible feeling, that deep-seeded insecurity I'd known all my life. Fear gripped me. I felt like I was fighting for my life, on the brink of disaster, about to lose everything we had worked so hard for. The pressure was so intense; it was as if my toes were on the edge of a cliff. I would look down, but I couldn't see anything. The ground was too far away, and my feet wouldn't move back from the cliff's edge. I knew it--we were about to fall off.

I blamed myself for everything.

I wanted someone to say to me, "It's going to be okay."

I desperately wanted to be saved.

I prayed to be rescued from this adversity. You may have prayed, written in journals, or practiced some type of religious or spiritual work when you've been in the darkest place. I would've done anything for God to miraculously eradicate my enemy, this amorphous, omnipresent, cultural force that seemed bent on ensuring my failure—I imagined He could, and He would. He should. Right?

Didn't God protect his children?

The rescue didn't come through though, and I became resentful toward God.

I felt lost and in despair, and I had a crisis of faith.

Why did all these bad things continue to happen to me?

Why did God make me this way?

Where's God now?

What I didn't realize in the thick of it was that this adversity was taking me deeper into my healing process and getting even deeper into the roots of my shame. It was taking me to a trauma that hadn't yet healed.

Oh, outwardly, I came across as I always had—results oriented and goal driven to those around me. I'd been perfecting this mask since that day in the judge's chamber. I knew that curled bangs and a neat barrette could do wonders to convince people nothing was wrong. Early on it was in the form of people pleasing and later manifested as more achievement oriented. My whole life, in fact, I'd been shielding my inner turmoil. Now, I felt my insides crumbling.

After agonizing deliberations, we decided to try to short sell the properties in 2009. Only, we couldn't sell anything. A $300,000 house wouldn't go for $99,000. At one point, a family friend advised us to take a hard look at all our financial options–-including filing for bankruptcy. Our financial advisor told us that this was exactly what bankruptcy was created for, but it didn't sit well with me or with Gary at the time.

One afternoon, our real estate agent stood in our living room and said with a straight face, "This is your fault. You signed the loan documents, and you can't file for bankruptcy."

That's when I lost it. My stress response was through the roof, and I lashed out at him.

"You're supposed to be working on our behalf," I said as my voice grew louder. "How dare you criticize us in our own living room! Who do you think you are, coming into our home and telling us what we can and can't do?"

The real estate agent looked dismayed, and he left our house silently.

Gary put his hand on my shoulder. "Why are you being so mean?" he asked gently. "It's not like you."

I sat down on our plush couch and sank into it, rocking myself back and forth, back and forth, with my knees tucked underneath my chin. I couldn't bear to see Gary's face and I couldn't bear him to see mine.

"I feel like I'm being assaulted on all fronts!"

It's YOUR FAULT! An internal voice screamed within me. *It's YOUR FAULT! YOUR FAULT!*

Suddenly, I was fifteen years old again. It's YOUR FAULT! I had told myself. You let them into your house. You let them drink your dad's beer. I was assaulted in my childhood home by teenage boys as they attempted to rape me. Three held me down while the fourth tried unsuccessfully to penetrate. I kicked and screamed and kept kicking and screaming. I remembered the assault vividly. I honestly thought I was going to die. The fighting paid off; I fought so hard the attackers stopped and scattered. But the assault stayed with me for decades to come. I told no one about this at the time, and I blamed myself.

It's YOUR FAULT! You drank beer too.

It's YOUR FAULT! You signed those loan documents too.

The past was alive in my brain, with all its terrible intensity. This experience in my living room triggered the self-blame and shame I carried all those years. I didn't call it this at the time, but it became a Bold Opportunity to Heal, the BOTH Approach-- in other words, **an opportunity to see current adversity as**

an opportunity to heal from a past trauma or adversity. The feelings that I experienced in the living room were real, yet felt so oddly out of proportion to what was currently happening with the real estate situation. That's what gave me a clue that something bigger was happening for me. As soon as I made the connection to the past event, my behavior suddenly made sense. My body had become overreactive to this type of threat-related signal. Feeling at fault for our financial losses at that moment and hearing the real estate agent's words of blame triggered my fight response related to the memory of the assault by those teenagers.

That experience long ago had forged in my mind a link between extreme survival circumstances and self-blame. Many men and women I've spoken to over the years have expressed something similar, particularly around traumatic events. Present-day events reactivate the raw feelings, and the biological signs of stress associated with events of the past. And they start telling themselves stories about themselves, like I did. "I keep getting myself in situations where I am re-living the feelings of the past." "I don't seem to be learning my lessons!" "I keep making the same mistakes over and over again."

As I rocked back and forth in the living room, my breath slowed. The calmer my breathing, the more grounded I became in time and space. I wasn't a teenager in that childhood bedroom. I wasn't being held down. I was in my home with my husband, decades later. As I looked around the room and looked toward Gary, I realized that this experience was an opportunity to heal the shame I'd carried all those years. Connecting both experiences made a deep and profound impact in my life that day. The experience of losing everything—the rental properties, our investments, retirement funds, etc.—helped me to also recognize what I did have: a loving husband, our house, and two children.

Mindset Shift: The circumstances I find myself in are not necessarily my fault; I can recognize the connections between my experiences.

The moment I made the connection between this event and my past adverse experience, I realized my Bold Opportunity to Heal. Consciously, I was able to tell my mind that this was not the same experience, and it was not my fault. I started to have compassion for myself in that moment, and for this exact trauma I had experienced. I gave my inner child a voice and told her it wasn't her fault. In that present moment, I told myself that the real estate crash wasn't my fault, and perhaps the whole situation could prove a valuable life lesson. Why was I so quick to assign blame and beat myself up about my decisions and their consequences rather than allow myself to experience pain and sadness?

Over the next few weeks, I became more mindful of how I carried my guilt. I also knew the importance of talking about this experience and its relatability to my past experiences to my support system, which included Gary. But mostly I was reckoning with this guilt and shame, and the false belief I had created about myself. None of that aligned with my true self or my intrinsic value. Guilt and shame were at the root of my self-loathing.

As adults, we have the capacity to make decisions and change our behaviors based upon our intrinsic value system. But it's more complicated than this.

The strongest commitment you can make right now is to behave consistently with your identity—who you are as a person matters, regardless of your experiences. Only sometimes, our true identities get obscured. Sometimes, just when we're about to put the cake in the oven, the dog starts barking her head off while your phone is blowing up, and the emails keep coming and we forget that the longer the cake sits, the more the batter will deflate. When you sustain a false belief system about who you are and what your intrinsic value is, you allow your behaviors to shift and change in negative ways. You lose alignment with your best self. And *mastering resilience*--well, that becomes nearly impossible.

Part of my brain needed to heal. I recognized that. I got to acknowledge who I truly was, and that meant reckoning with all that guilt and shame and blame. I was no more at fault for the circumstances at fifteen years old than fifty. To see that, I got to see the story I'd been telling myself was just that--a story I'd been clutching for dear life.

Taking my fifteen-year-old perspective and reframing the experience was incredibly important. I was able to see from the perspective of my younger self, but I also acknowledged that I could reimagine my inner child's story. In this way, I leaned into my healing journey.

Over and over again, I repeated to myself, neither of these events were your fault.

I came to a crucial realization. My current circumstances and struggles were helping me heal my past adversities. When this occurred, I knew I had an opportunity to take advantage of this personal Bold Opportunity to Heal. I accepted what had happened to my fifteen-year-old self, and acknowledged that it was a horrendous experience, yet I could also see that my current adversity was facilitating this past healing. Going through tough present circumstances allowed me to heal from past wounds. This helped me build my resilience muscle.

Mindset Shift: My current circumstances and struggles help me to heal my past adversities.

I want you to now ask yourself, "Who have I become in the face of more recent adversity?"

Back in those perilous days of 2008 and 2009, one of my mentors said, "You are a butterfly."

I tried to embrace the metaphor. I imagined myself wrapped tight in a cocoon. But instead of feeling warmth and comfort, I felt trapped and distraught. This is how I came to realize that all those rescue fantasies were best left fantasies. If I had been rescued by God, Gary or anyone else, I wouldn't have experienced my own personal transformation. I wouldn't have learned, once again, how the pain and struggle of adversity transforms us into something more than we ever could've imagined.

Caterpillars are born with everything necessary to become butterflies. All their genetic code is stored in their cells, waiting to be unlocked. The chrysalis protects the caterpillar as it becomes a liquid, gooey substance before it can transform into a butterfly, which then pushes against the walls of the chrysalis, building the strength to fly. This struggle is a necessary part of metamorphosis. Cut open the cocoon during this process and the butterfly dies. It doesn't have a chance to see the light of the sun, or meet the resplendent, fragrant beauty of nectar-rich flowers. Had I been rescued, I would not have transformed into the better version of myself, healed from the blame and shame of a traumatic event from the past.

Some of you may still be in the hard shell of the chrysalis, feeling stuck. Some of you may be in the very first part of the transformation, feeling uncertain about your present and your future, wondering what else there is to your life. Some of you are in the heat of the struggle, continuously fighting to release your old shell to become a better version of yourself. And some of you are drying your wings, pausing before take-off.

Then, there are those of you who are already transformed. You're ready to fly. You're feeling free to live authentically in the present moment.

No matter where you are in this transformation process, recognize that **you are on your own healing journey**. It does not serve you to compare your journey to mine or anyone else's. You are right where you're supposed to be. Each step in this process is necessary to complete to further your healing.

Mindset Shift: I am right where I'm supposed to be on my healing journey.

While we go on these beautiful and complicated healing journeys, please take a moment to recognize that change is often hard. If you're constantly working, like Alex and Emma, taking care of students or children in different environments, you may be wondering what everyone else thinks of you. You may still be in a "people-pleasing" mode of living your life. You may wonder if your support system will still love you if you do change. It's so easy to make yourself feel inadequate.

I encourage you to feel powerful.

I encourage you to feel successful.

I encourage you to say aloud, "My circumstances are not my fault."

I encourage you to recognize that you are no longer a victim of your past circumstances or past adversities.

Through understanding the root of my own insecurities and self-loathing, I connected the dots. For the first time, I was able to get out of my comfort zone, which meant leaving the dark places my mind had wandered for so many years.

Mindset Shift: My circumstances or past adversities will no longer make me feel inadequate.

When you realize you do have control over your circumstances, you know you're stepping into the right direction. Over the years, I've spoken to many people about their own adversities, not only in childhood, but also in adulthood. I would hear things like:

"The world is out to get me."

"I feel paranoid constantly."

"I feel like my coworkers are always snickering behind my back."

"I don't feel adequately prepared as a parent/teacher."

These feelings can become relentless and overwhelming. We recognize that adversity can be bad, yet we also recognize that good can come out of these experiences––and that notion is reassuring.

We can choose to believe things are against us just as easily as we can believe things are for us. It's that simple. We can be paranoid, or we can choose to experience "pronoia," paranoia's opposite, the belief that the world around us conspires to benefit us. The universal law of reciprocity reveals that all laws must reciprocate mutually with each other. In other words, if we believe the world is out to get us, it is equally true that the world is for us. The brain doesn't know the difference between real and imagined. We can choose to believe things are for us, just as easily as we can believe things are against us. It's that simple. Rewrite the story in your favor.

Mindset Shift: My circumstances happen for me, not to me or against me.

The onslaught of adversity I experienced in 2008-2009 was a huge turning point in my healing journey. While shifting my perspective on these events, I realized, after much work and dedication, that I was not to blame for what had happened to me as a teenager. Not only did I have more compassion for myself, but for the first time in my life, I also experienced true forgiveness. I attributed that to current events initiating a Bold Opportunity to Heal from past adversity.

No matter what age you are, you can also experience this experience of healing the past through the current events. Remember to incorporate all the ingredients of the recipe--commitment, clarity of self, and compassion (for yourself and others) and as you use the AAAs of Mastering Resilience, then fold in the secret sauce, the BOTH Approach, to Mastering Resilience, which all blends together in your ultimate healing journey. You are not to blame for your adverse experiences, yet you cannot change the past. You can work on yourself through therapy, mindset shifts, a host of other positive healing strategies and self-help tools to get to a point of recognizing your true identity and how your behavior can be in alignment with your intrinsic value.

I didn't have this realization until I turned fifty years old.

While other situations in adulthood had posed similar challenges, this one dramatically changed me--for the better. During my healing, I knew that dealing with the real estate broker, confronting the lack of retirement funds, and even weighing bankruptcy would ultimately serve a greater purpose in my life. And it did.

While I'm still susceptible to bouts of self-criticism, now I have a process to counteract those negative thoughts, so they don't control me. There are moments where I question, and then I say, "No, I am confident." At night, when I wake up ruminating, I go through the AAAs; I practice through the BOTH Approach. I get to do some more work. Even if I wanted to, I couldn't go back to my old hiding place. I've recognized too much of my beautiful self and my intrinsic value. My resilience muscle grows stronger every day.

In the face of adversity, we can feel triggered, lingering on familiar past feelings. Yet once we recognize the pattern, we can become like beautiful butterflies while making a difference in the world, and creating a greater ripple effect for those surrounding us.

Mindset Shift: The sum of my circumstances has made me who I am today.

As you continue to acknowledge who you are and behave in ways consistent with this identity, living authentically and in integrity, consistent with your purpose, will become easier. When you live as your best self, you have more capacity in your life to master resilience and transform what happened to you into the positive impact you are meant to have in the world.

*   *   *

This approach is the secret to sustaining lasting results of the work you put into your own healing journey. But Emma didn't think so. When explaining the BOTH Approach to her at brunch one morning, I noticed her nodding along with what I was saying.

"The BOTH Approach is a simple process," I said. "Spending time rehashing the past without shifting our perspectives is unhelpful at best and damaging at worst. We're not going to achieve major breakthroughs in our lives or in our careers if we're unable to see the good that came out of our adverse experiences."

Emma nodded again, looking down at her plate of banana pancakes. You know, I used to hate banana pancakes," she said wistfully, swirling her fork around the plate. "My dad made my siblings and me banana pancakes before he left us. And I resented banana pancakes because they reminded me so much of him. In college, though, my friends would get loads of different kinds of pancakes at the diner on Sunday mornings. My friend, Lindsey, and the others used to rave about their banana pancakes. They always asked me why I wouldn't try them, and I always made some odd excuse. It took me fifteen years, but I finally worked up the courage to try a bite once again. But, Lorry, after one bite that time, I couldn't stomach any more. Banana pancakes were my favorite when I was little, but I actually hated them in college. How could I have let a stupid memory color my tastes? But I did, and it still does to some extent. I guess I was feeling brave today when ordering them," she said. "Aha." No wonder Emma hadn't taken more than a couple bites of her breakfast. "Emma, that's not a stupid memory at all," I said. "Let's reframe the whole situation. Do you have any fond memories of those Saturday mornings with your dad and your siblings? It may be difficult to decipher between your hurt feelings and any positive memories but try to think." "Well, when I think about it," she said slowly, "I *do* remember laughing a lot at the table. It's one of the few times we resembled a happy family." "That's fantastic! Now you have an opportunity to shift perspective here. You can acknowledge what your dad did—leaving you—and acknowledge how much that hurt you. Yet, what if it's okay to like banana pancakes because they're delicious AND because they're part of this family memory? Could you start to fully enjoy banana pancakes again? Can we look at this as a positive memory, an opportunity to heal?" Tears welled up in Emma's eyes underneath her red-framed glasses. "Excuse me," she said softly, and disappeared into the bathroom. She came out several minutes later with bloodshot eyes and flushed cheeks. But she was smiling. "Okay, Lorry, I'll start to look at this as an opportunity to heal. I do want this for myself, but it's incredibly difficult to see the good when there was so much bad. Does that even make sense?" "Of course, Emma," I looked into her eyes. "It makes perfect sense." Emma smiled again, picked up her fork, and took a bite. "These really are delicious." Our adversities are what make us who we are. Our adversities are what make us drawn to heal the next generation. By the same token, our adversities are often what continue to trigger us. When we continue to behave in reaction to those triggers, it's evidence that we have some deeper healing to do. We are responsible—regardless of our age, our identity, our income level, or whatever circumstances we may find ourselves in—to do the inner work to heal ourselves and heal the negative aspects of our past experiences in order to give those in our care the freedom to do the same. Focusing on the negative doesn't serve us. Our focus on the negative is what keeps us in the victim mentality. That energy it takes to maintain our victimhood keeps us prisoners of the past. During your healing process, acknowledge the hurt you felt while also being mindful and intentional about any positivity that has come from your past (when you're ready). Also, continue to do more activities and have more experiences that are good for you. I want your good qualities to develop even further.

There are ways to showcase gratitude, even in tumultuous times. By taking a deeper dive into The BOTH Approach, you can make a conscious choice about what to do with this new information. Recognize how you once perceived an adverse experience and how you can reframe it. Healing yourself has a snowball effect. Healing yourself fuels your future goals and dreams.

Emma often thought about the childhood she didn't have. She had friends who went on family vacations twice a year, ate dinner with both parents, and had a stable home environment. In college, she met people whose first move had been into the dorm. At that point, Emma had lost count of how many times she had moved, and only two items remained from her childhood: a stuffed dog named Brownie, and her favorite picture book, *Guess How Much I Love You*. Emma remembered these items coming from a Christmas donation by kind strangers. Meanwhile, her college friends complained about going through their childhood artwork. They had "too many family photo albums" to scan. Emma longed for their problems. She wished she had a "normal" childhood, not one of despair, confusion, and instability.

After the banana pancakes that morning, we talked more about Emma's childhood.

"I just wish I had those same 'problems' that my other friends had," she said solemnly. "I think about those friends still and wonder how they're getting along."

"Emma, it's okay to mourn your childhood and wish for something different. That's part of the healing process..." I shook my head. "The reality is, no amount of healing will ever take away the fact that your childhood was lived ... like that. Your childhood can't be rewritten or redone."

We sat in silence for a moment before I continued, letting her digest this information.

"You can acknowledge the childhood you had while simultaneously understanding that you can do something more about it," I added. "You can heal your inner child who lived through abandonment and through other adversities. You get to do this when you connect your current experiences to circumstances in the past--this is what allows you to heal. Not all Bold Opportunities to Heal need to be seeped in current traumatic experiences. Some can be as easy as beginning to enjoy banana pancakes again."

CHAPTER NINE

Consider Possibilities: Stay Out of Your Comfort Zone + Course Corrections

Our goals can only be reached through a vehicle of a plan, in which we must fervently believe, and upon which we must vigorously act. There is no other route to success.

—Pablo Picasso

The COVID-19 pandemic wreaked havoc on global mental health, especially in youth populations. A review of many articles published in *Child and Adolescent Mental Health* one year into the pandemic reported rates of suicidal ideation, suicide, and self-injury increased; neurodiverse children, youth with pre-existing mental health issues, and children with chronic physical health conditions "experienced higher levels of psychological distress, depression, anxiety, and behavior problems" (Samji et al., 2021). As we do our own work toward Mastering Resilience, we move closer to more totally meeting the needs of youth in a psychological state of crisis.

*   *   *

When I first stepped into my role as leader in the non-profit sector, I knew I was going to do more public speaking. I was a wreck. I was a complete ball of nerves on stage or talking to groups of people. I had taught college and graduate school classes and yet I still feared speaking in public. If you had asked my friends and family, they would've said, "Lorry can talk your ear off! She's an excellent communicator!" Yet when it came to speaking on the stage in front of groups of strangers, I lost my wits. I was very anxious and afraid of making a fool of myself.

A colleague suggested that I take an improv class, one designed for executives to overcome their fear of public speaking. That first day, I walked into the room, utterly terrified. Looking around, I saw other prominent executive level leaders, and for the first time since becoming an executive in leadership, I didn't feel alone.

One of the initial exercises in this class was to make a fool of ourselves, on stage, on purpose. We were asked to think of our most embarrassing moment and create a comedy routine around it. For me, my most embarrassing moment was easy to recall. When I was just a newly licensed psychologist, I was volunteering at a low-cost counseling clinic. The director was going on a mini-vacation and asked me to cover for her while she was out.

I was feeling the confidence of being newly licensed and of being trusted to be in charge. One of the projects during her absence was the installation of a new phone system. I took the management of this project quite seriously. The phone maintenance person arrived, and he immediately made very direct, intense eye contact when I met him in the waiting room of the clinic.

Ah, he is acknowledging that I am the one in charge, I thought.

As we navigated through the offices, I bent down to show him where the phone jacks were so that he could install the new phones in the correct spots. He continued to make very solid eye contact throughout the entire tour of the office. I falsely attributed it to his honoring the position of leadership I was in, covering for the director of the clinic and all. What he didn't tell me, nor anyone else for that matter, was that when I had emerged from the bathroom earlier in the day, I had tucked my skirt into my stockings. Not just a little bit. I'd pulled the entire back side of my stockings over the back of my skirt. His eye contact had nothing to do with my being in charge--he was trying not to look at my exposed rear end. It was a story that I had not told often, but one that made me laugh every time. If not from the embarrassment of it, but for the sheer lesson in humility that I got to learn early on in my career. I thought up to that point that I'd been humbled enough, but apparently not.

As everyone went around the room, embarrassing themselves on purpose, we all became more comfortable with each other-- and with the idea of being ourselves. The class ended with a live show for our friends and family and a few random audience members who frequented the theater. Taking this improv class improved my public speaking skills dramatically—not because I needed help pausing, or with my posture, but because I got to experience stepping well outside my comfort zone to be a better version of myself.

Early in my work life, I'd considered the possibilities of my career trajectory. I'd set the goal to be the leader of a non-profit, and I wanted to be great at it. It meant that I got to step out of my comfort zone and stay there.

When you become open, and stay open, to consider new possibilities, you allow the right people, situations, and paths to come into your life easily and graciously. You'll soon be able to vividly imagine how your goals can fit into this new life path. Focus, determination, and attraction are the key ingredients here.

In our comfort zones, whether we like it or not, we are at the status quo. We may feel we're living on automatic pilot. Some of us get up at the same time every day, complete our morning routine, go to work, come home, put the kids to bed, and watch TV before doing the same thing the very next day. And the next. And the next. We get so used to routines and our comfort zones that we may not realize that those routines are numbing us. Many people who have experienced adversity choose to live this way. They are simply getting by because it's a safer option. It feels safe to be in a comfortable place in life, where they know what's going to happen that day and the next day. Others may call this kind of life "boring," but if you grew up with ACEs and flinched every time you heard a noise, you'll understand the appeal of a quiet, safe routine.

Imagine your comfort zone as your home. You may live in a house, an apartment, a condo, a townhouse, or somewhere else entirely. Wherever you live, I want you to close your eyes, and see yourself within the walls of your home.

Now, in this vision, open the front door and take one step forward, closing the door behind you. Look around and observe what you see and how you feel.

Moving out of your own comfort zone doesn't require you to go bungee jumping or skydiving tomorrow, and it doesn't have to involve telling the public about your most embarrassing moment. In fact, it's the exact opposite. When you step out of your comfort zone, you're taking one step. Just one step. Not to the next street, not to the front or backyard, but one step. Consider the possibilities means ultimately setting a goal, and then taking one step in the direction of that goal that you set for yourself.

Consider how stepping outside your front door, just with one step, can help you reach your goal while being the best version of yourself. Will you be kinder to yourself? To others? Will you eat differently? Will you go for that promotion at work? Will you start volunteering at your local animal shelter because your partner is allergic to cats, but you love cats and want to be around cats once a week?

Also, consider who you get to be to step into your ideal future and your higher self. Understanding your intrinsic value is just as important as setting goals, creating a plan, visualizing these goals, and then achieving them.

You've committed to this healing journey and toward being the best version of yourself. You've already established your BIG Why and your Why NOW. You now understand your own intrinsic value. You know how to behave in alignment with your true identity. When behaving in this way, your *false-self* floats away as silently as a cloud on a sunny day. It's important, of course, to always remember your new, positive behaviors rather than your old, negative thoughts that someone may have implanted into your head as a young child. If your old patterns return--and they may throughout your life--always remember to visualize your BIG Why and your Why NOW to motivate you to keep going, and use the AAAs of mastering resilience whenever you feel stuck.

*   *   *

Groups I've spoken to--whether youth themselves or leaders and influencers of youth, clients, supervisees, and those I've mentored--find these five steps to be very helpful when considering their own possibilities:

Step One: Dream

> *Without leaps of imagination or dreaming, we lose*
> *the excitement of possibilities. Dreaming, after all,*
> *is a form of planning.*
>
> —*Gloria Steinem*

Keep in mind what you've been learning about yourself, including your tendencies and your behaviors. Dream about infinite possibilities that are in complete alignment with your higher self and your BIG Why. These dreams put you on a beautiful, perfect trajectory for your life.

If you feel drawn to complete a visualization exercise, try this one. Close your eyes, and get into a comfortable position on your chair. Make sure your shoulders are back, and you're sitting up straight. Imagine that you're on an island. What do you see? Hear? Smell? Taste? Touch? Who are you with, if anyone? What job do you have? Where are you going to school? This unbelievably gorgeous island represents the ideal life you want. Continue to imagine where your path will take you a year from now, then five years from now, and ten years from now. Allow yourself to see anything and everything that you've ever wanted on this island. Fear may come up in this visualization exercise. If it does, acknowledge the fear and continue to visualize this dream of yours. Here, success is the only option, and money is no object. Your desires are here, perfect and beautiful, just the way they are. This island is a pure representation of the ideal life you want—the ideal life you deserve to have.

Step Two: Set a Goal

*By recording your dreams and goals on paper, you set
in motion the process of becoming the person you most
want to be. Put your future in good hands—your own.*

—*Mark Victor Hansen*

You may want to get a new job. You may want to write your book. You may want to change your business to attract different types of clients. Or you may simply want to set more boundaries in your personal life. When we talk about stepping out of your comfort zone, it's important to consider what it means to take one step in that direction of the new goal you set for yourself, and how this new goal is in complete alignment with your intrinsic value and ultimately, your purpose. A very important part of setting the goal is declaring it complete, and visualizing it as complete, as if it is already achieved—as you'll see later.

Researchers have understood the power of goal setting in the workplace for decades (Pritchard et al., 1988). Thousands of companies around the world use goal setting in some form, including Coca Cola Company, PricewaterhouseCoopers International Ltd., Nike Inc., Intel Corporation, and Microsoft Corporation. Goal setting helps motivate athletes, entrepreneurs, and individuals to achieve at higher levels of difficulty.

A critical first step in obtaining a new goal is to write it down. Written goals allow you to declare the destination and provide a map where you can chart your effort; they help you see whether you're heading in the right direction. When we write down our goals, we're able to store this information within a specific location: in your phone, on the computer, on a notecard. There's also a biological process that occurs when we write down our goals called encoding, where things we perceive in life travel to our brain's hippocampus, which analyzes new pieces of information. Decisions are made regarding what items get stored in our long-term memory and which ones become discarded. When we write our goals, this ultimately improves the encoding process. We're more likely to remember the goals long-term (Forbes).

Goal setting is also extremely motivating, especially when you're able to physically look at a sheet of paper with these goals written down daily. When we set goals and are motivated by them, we become encouraged to develop new techniques and skills to achieve these goals we set for ourselves (Latham & Locke, 2001). Whether you're a teacher, a counselor, a parent, or even an entrepreneur, understanding how to reach your goal is the crucial next step.

When you are goal-oriented, you become more resourceful. Your problem-solving skills increase, and you have a higher capacity of being able to "figure it out" if you're unsure of how to obtain the next step in achieving your goal. Resourcefulness involves planning, strategizing, prioritizing, seeking outside resources, and monitoring your progress. These important skills will lead you on your path to being committed to your goal.

After you write down your goals, visualize one. Remember, our brains are rewireable due to neuroplasticity. By meditating, visualizing, and asking questions, feeling the emotion of achieving these goals, we can enhance the growth of our brains. In 2012, researchers from Harvard University and the University of Auckland found the human brain isn't always able to distinguish between a memory of the past and a vision of the future (Schacter et.al).

Let's look at a couple of prominent examples.

In a Harvard Medical School study, two groups of people learned to play the piano. Both groups were instructed how to play a scale one-handed by neuroscientist Alvaro Pascual-Leone.

For five days straight, Group A practiced the scale on the piano every day for two hours daily. Meanwhile, Group B imagined practicing the scale on the piano for two hours every day. Each group had their brains scanned by transcranial-magnetic-stimulation (TMS), which allows scientists to see how the neurons in the brain are functioning beneath the coil. Participants in *both* groups were able to sit and play this scale after one week, even though Group B hadn't practiced the scale like Group A had. When the brain imaging came back, the conductors of the study were amazed—it revealed changes in the brain that reflected permanent learning. This study confirmed that **by practicing a skill mentally, we have the power to change the physical structure of our brains.**

Mindset Shift: I imagine and visualize my goals to achieve them.

In sports, the act of imagining, or visualizing, one's capabilities is critical to athletes' success. In a *Psychology Today* interview, Richard Suinn, Ph.D., the first psychologist to serve on a US Olympic sports medicine team, discusses the particular strategy athletes have for managing their stress:

> The first thing that athletes do in dealing with their stress is to identify what triggers it. For some people it's a particular environment in which they find themselves; for others it's certain words that people use. The second step is to be aware of how they react when they're under stress. Sometimes they have a physiological reaction, such as sweaty palms or an elevated heart rate. In that case, we have them use biofeedback or relaxation

training. Prevention is even better: if they know that they're going to face a stressful situation, they can engage in some relaxation procedures beforehand... Mental practice is also referred to as 'visualization' or 'imagery rehearsal.' We start with twenty to thirty minutes of relaxation training, followed by the visualization of some aspect of the athlete's game that can be improved. It's the mental equivalent of physical practice. For instance, if your golf swing is a little off and your coach shows you the proper swing, then during visualization you practice making that correct swing in your mind. It may be that your muscles start to learn through this visualizing practice the proper way of moving. There is, in fact, research evidence that indicates that when athletes use visualization after relaxation, their performance does improve.

In fact, a study conducted by researchers in the Department of Biomedical Engineering at the Cleveland Clinic published in the journal *Neuropsychologia* found that, in strength training, "mental practice" increased muscle strength by 35 percent. While physical practice increased muscle strength by 53 percent, mental practice also provided the added benefit of enhanced cortical potential, a measure related to muscle control.

No wonder visualization is so critical to achieving your ultimate goals and mastering resilience. As you can see, setting a goal and visualizing this goal better prepares you to achieve what you set out to do. Stepping out of your comfort zone can be difficult, but it can also be extremely rewarding.

So, how do you begin visualizing?

Step Three: Make a Plan

Give me six hours to chop down a tree and I will spend the first four sharpening the ax.

—*Abraham Lincoln*

Visualizing your goals hugely impacts your likelihood of achieving them. The next step is to make a plan of action, where you'll identify a road map and learn how this goal can truly become your reality. Think about your BIG Why, the reason you're setting that goal. Your BIG Why is the context for this goal. The visualization of achieving that goal in the context of your BIG Why and your motivation to achieve it--your Why NOW--helps you take that first step. What action step can you take to move you in the direction of your goal? What plan will ultimately help you achieve your goal?

Throughout this phase of your healing journey, you'll map out a course. Imagine you were planning a road trip across the continental United States. If you start in San Francisco and want to end up in New York City, you need to understand how long the trip will take, where you'll stay along the way, and what sights you want to explore throughout the trip. It won't be perfect, though. You may take a wrong turn and arrive later than you hoped. You may drive through snow or rain. The hotel may be overbooked. The restaurant you chose may be out of your favorite dish. All of this is okay because you're setting yourself up for success by understanding the basic path that will get you to your destination.

In 2001, researchers in Great Britain took 248 people to build better exercise habits over two weeks (Sarah Milne, 2002).

The researchers created three groups. Group One represented the control group, where individuals were asked to track how often they exercised. Group Two was the motivation group. They were asked to track their exercise habits and read material on the benefits of exercise. This group also learned that exercise could potentially reduce the risk of coronary heart disease and improve heart health. Group Three received the same presentation as Group Two. Additionally, Group Three was asked to devise a plan for when and where they'd exercise over the course of the following week. They were instructed to complete the following sentence, "During the next week, I will partake in at least twenty minutes of vigorous exercise on [DAY] at [TIME]."

Group One and Group Two had similar results; 35 to 38 percent of those individuals exercised at least once per week. However, 91 percent of Group Three exercised at least once per week, which was more than double the normal rate.

Writing down their plan of action improved their results dramatically, and they were more likely to follow through with their goals. Psychologists call these specific plans "implementation intentions." They state when, where, and how you intend to implement a particular behavior. Implementation intentions have been used to work through four potential problems for goal pursuit: failing to get started, becoming rigid, getting derailed, and overextending oneself.

These findings have been repeated across hundreds of studies and have been found to increase the odds that people will start exercising, begin recycling, stick with studying, and even stop smoking.

Think about a time when you accomplished a task. If your first thought is, "I've never accomplished anything," think again. Did you learn the alphabet? Did you figure out how to ride a bike? Did you get your GED? Did you graduate from college? Make a list of all your accomplishments, and don't be shy. Don't be afraid to write these down, either. Crossing the climbing frame in fifth grade counts as an accomplishment too.

Now pick one accomplishment from your list. How did you complete this? Did it take guts and willpower? Perseverance? How exactly did you accomplish this amazing feat? Were you working alone? Did you have help? Did you delegate it? Write down the answers to these questions and start noticing the steps it took to achieve all you've already accomplished in your life.

You achieve goals all the time, even when you don't call them "goals." Think about it. You take out the trash. You cook a meal. You wash dishes. You get dressed. When you make a practice of giving yourself credit for these small yet mighty accomplishments, you'll soon start to see how these small steps can help you create the plan to get to your "BIG Why," along your journey to mastering resilience.

It's important to note that these small steps may already be well within your comfort zone. To reach your full potential, remember that it's imperative to step out of your comfort zone to reach your true purpose, and to live your life according to your intrinsic values. When you create your plan, your first step, or second step, may be out of your comfort zone initially—and that's okay. Think about what going out of your comfort zone means for you personally. Every individual is on a unique and beautiful trajectory, including you.

Step Four: Establish Personal Responsibility and Accountability

Interested people do what is easy and convenient. Committed people upgrade their identity to match the destiny they want. They upgrade their beliefs, their habits, and their skills to match the goals and dreams they are committed to achieving. They do whatever it takes.

—John Assaraf

You've declared your goal. You've written down your goal. You've established a plan to achieve your goal. Perhaps you've even told your support network about your goal. Now it's time to take personal responsibility and establish accountability to achieve your goal in alignment with your true self. Be true to your word

Continue to be 100 percent committed to your journey and your ultimate goal. And acknowledge your progress, as well; if you wanted to get an *A* on your last test, but you received a *B*, understand that you worked hard to achieve that *B*. Celebrate this success; after all, it's a step in your journey. On the other hand, if you set the goal to get an *A* and then got a *B* because you didn't complete all the assignments leading up to the test and didn't study, that's even more reason to celebrate the grade, because it could have been worse. Then you get to assess your level of personal responsibility and accountability as a factor in whether you achieved your goal.

Understanding that things may not go according to your plan is a critical part of your journey. So is developing agility, which you'll need when it's time to correct your course of action.

When I'm interviewing candidates for a job, one of my favorite questions to ask is, "What's a serious mistake you've made and what did you do to reconcile it?" On rare occasions, the candidate thinks for half a second and says, "I can't remember the last time I made a serious mistake." I know the question might catch them off guard because we don't tend to want to lead with our mistakes, especially in the context of a job interview. And, truth be told, some people don't have the ability to get so vulnerable. It can be embarrassing. It can be uncomfortable. Yet, when we acknowledge our missteps, we allow for an openness to learning from those missteps. We can make course corrections. And sometimes our missteps even help us establish accountability to ourselves. They show us our true potential and how our intrinsic value plays a role in reaching our goal.

Missteps can benefit our success. We get to admit to ourselves that everybody makes mistakes, that we make mistakes, and that it's okay. You have the capacity to control your behavior and to make choices in alignment with your dreams and goals. The little choices we make daily—what we eat, how we treat ourselves, what we say to others, and so much more—all play a part in reaching your goals. For example, if you set a goal to release weight and then choose to eat a cheesecake every day, you're probably doing yourself a disservice and hindering your ability to meet that ultimate goal. On the other hand, if you set the goal to release weight and for the most part you eat healthy--on the rare occasion enjoying a piece of cheesecake-- you can tell yourself, "That was delicious!" and get back on track. A steady series of choices in the direction of your dreams and goals will make it more likely that you'll achieve them in the long run.

One of the questions I ask myself and others about a goal is, "How serious are you about achieving this goal of yours?" Stop in the moment and ask yourself, "Am I where I want to be?" If your immediate answer is 'no,' it might be time to make a different choice. Choose a different direction. What we tell ourselves matters, and our inner voice can help us--or deter us--from staying on course.

When I was in my twenties, I had a very clear goal to get a Ph.D. I was working multiple jobs while attending graduate school. I was a successful student, but I felt fragmented and like a fraud because of specific choices I made to numb myself: fast motorcycle rides from boyfriends, drugs, and more. Many of my decisions were self-destructive, and I thought, at the time, that they reflected my true self.

I was mistaken.

I was listening to my inner critic, who kept telling me failure was my fate. I felt victimized by any situation that didn't go my way and took everything personally. I so badly wanted to please others; I couldn't fathom putting my own needs first. I wanted to be liked and loved by everyone besides myself.

One day after partying the night before, I called in sick to work. At that point, I had to ask myself, "If I keep making these choices, will I reach my goal?"

The obvious answer was 'no.'

From then on, I followed the steps outlined above while maintaining my values along the way. I also sought out mentors and a support system that could help me.

I remember once working on a dissertation proposal about Adult Children of Alcoholics. I couldn't seem to get it off the ground. I was triggered by the subject and decided to completely change my dissertation topic. I was interested in a concept called metacognition (simply put, thinking about one's thinking) and decided to write a dissertation proposal about that topic. I introduced myself to a professor with expertise in metacognition and asked him for guidance. Though he'd never met me, he gave me an assignment to read and told me to come back and see him when I finished. I did as he suggested; he gave me another assignment to read, as well as specific action steps to take between appointments with him. He told me to introduce myself to other experts in metacognition and learn about their work. He agreed to chair my dissertation committee. We created a plan together to complete my dissertation research, with built-in accountability to earn my degree. Each time we met, I asked him what steps I needed to take between meetings to further my dissertation research and to move it closer to completion. Eventually, he suggested that I didn't need to be told what to do, but still I insisted on verbalizing the steps I would take before our next scheduled meeting. I feared that if left to my own devises I was less likely to get things done. I didn't trust my own motivation yet. It was that accountability of agreeing to specific action steps, telling someone else what I was going to do, and then following through that ensured I achieved my goal of completing my Ph.D.

Step 5: Trust Your Tendencies

Whether you think you can, or you think you can't—
you're right.

—Henry Ford

As you build in accountability to your plan to achieve your goal, it's important to first understand and then trust your tendencies. One of my favorite authors, Gretchen Rubin, has a quiz called The Four Tendencies. On the quiz, she asks a simple question, "How do I respond to expectations?" There are two kinds of prominent expectations: outer (meeting deadlines, responding to a text message, etc.) and inner (lose forty pounds, begin a meditation practice, etc.). Our responses to these expectations determine which tendency we fall under—Upholder, Questioner, Obliger, or Rebel.

According to Rubin, Upholders want to know what should be done; they build in both internal and external accountability to rock their goals. Obligers need accountability. As an Obliger, it's imperative to have an accountability buddy and make commitments to others. Share these with a supportive friend. You're more likely to commit to others than you are to yourself. Questioners want justifications. Make sure to have all the information you need ahead of time to meet your inner expectations if you're a Questioner. Rebels want freedom to do things their own way. As a Rebel, it's critical to have goals that are meaningful enough to keep you motivated; be sure to build in a structure that's easy and fun to follow.

When we know our tendency, we have more information about how best to make promises to ourselves and keep them. As Rubin writes, "The Four Tendencies explain why we act and why we don't act." Armed with this self-knowledge, we can become less stressed, more engaged with others, and better equipped to make decisions in line with our intrinsic value. And, importantly, knowing your tendency allows you to determine what kind of accountability works for you. Above all, no matter your tendency, understand your expected results clearly and build in celebrations along the way. Continue to be wholly committed to your journey and your goal.

*   *   *

After Emma and I had been meeting regularly for months, she had an epiphany about her comfort zone and her next goal. The sun was shining, and we were both wearing hats and sunglasses.

Emma was sipping her decaf chai. "Lorry, I think I've been in this place for so long where I'm comfortable with my daily routine. It's not a bad thing, but now I'm wondering what's next for me. You know, a coworker mentioned that she's doing a graduate school program at night. She said our district would increase our pay if we got a master's degree as well, so that's something I'm considering. It just sounds daunting, to be honest."

"I see how that could sound hard," I said, "but sometimes we get to push ourselves outside our comfort zone, sometimes it's literally one step at a time, to achieve our next big goal in life. Going to graduate school could be a really great next step for you."

"I suppose," she sighed. "I'm just not sure how it'd work with my current schedule, and I already have so many loans I'm paying off from undergrad."

"What would happen if you looked at graduate programs and just applied?" I asked. "No strings attached. The first step is to apply and see what happens. How does that sound?"

"It sounds uncomfortable, but it also doesn't sound as daunting as what my coworker described," she said, her breath slowing down. "I suppose I could try and see what happens."

"That's great, Emma!" I reached over and squeezed her hand. "That's something to be proud of!"

CHAPTER TEN

Connections
& Close Relationships

Surround yourself with people who don't just ask how
you are doing. Surround yourself with people who make
an effort to make sure they are part of the reason you
are doing so well.

—*Jennae Cecelia, Uncaged Wallflower*

Positive, trusting relationships with adults are essential for children, especially children with ACEs. In a 2018 study examining such relationships among children in residential care, researchers at Australian Catholic University observed "Children and young people...place importance on the need for consistent, reliable, strong, and lasting relationships with trusted workers and recognize the therapeutic value of doing so."

We are called to be consistent, reliable, strong, and supportive for the youth we work with and care for. We need them too. This is our truth.

*　　　*　　　*

When Alex walked into my office with a solemn look on his face, I knew he wanted to talk about something important. At this point, Alex had been working with me for about eight months. We'd had dozens of weekly meetings. We discussed his cases, of course, and he also shared elements of his personal life, especially when it directly or indirectly impacted his work with clients.

I looked him in the eyes, waiting for him to talk. I didn't need to ask what was on his mind. I knew he wanted to express himself.

"Lorry, I broke up with my girlfriend last night." He released an enormous sigh. "As you may remember, we had been together for two years. It took me such a long time to realize this, but I want a true partner in my life. I felt like I was doing the heavy lifting at home. We started living together a year ago, but I always did everything—the cooking, the cleaning, paying bills. Hell, I know she makes more money than I do, and she never offered to pay more than half for rent ... I really do love her, but I didn't feel I could be my authentic self with her. She made me feel badly for wanting to become a therapist. See, everyone in her family is a lawyer, and she went to law school and passed the bar, too, but that's not my path. I always felt pushed to be someone who I wasn't, and I want to find a partner who believes in me and believes in my goals I'm setting for myself."

I let him pause and gather himself.

"Alex, first of all, thank you for sharing this with me," I said. "This isn't an easy realization to come to, and I'm sorry you're going through this breakup."

Alex nodded.

"I miss her already, if I'm honest with myself," he said. "The relationship had a lot of positive qualities. We made so many memories together—vacations, weddings, birthdays—my nephew started calling her 'Auntie' a few months ago."

"That's a completely normal reaction."

"Thanks, Lorry...I guess I felt I couldn't really be my true self around her, and I'm finally able to understand that, as sad as it seems right now."

Years later, Alex would call me and tell me he was engaged to the woman of his dreams. She supported him wholeheartedly, and he, in turn, supported her work as a veterinarian. I was elated to receive this phone call, even though we hadn't been in touch in quite a while. I knew that Alex was on his right path, and he was in complete alignment with his intrinsic value in terms of his relationship.

*   *   *

One of my favorite ingredients in this Mastering Resilience journey--the icing on the cake, so to speak--is nurturing meaningful connections and close relationships. I've been blessed with having very deep and lasting relationships in my lifetime with people who love and care about me. I'm surrounded by people who honor my freedom to be genuinely who I am created to be, who bring out the best version of me when I'm with them, who hold space for my feelings and my tears, who understand my anxiety and my triggers, and who love me as I am, with all my imperfections. I can be completely vulnerable with those closest to me. When I share my dreams and goals, they root me on like a cheer squad. They applaud my accomplishments and sit with me in my life lessons—when I'm making course corrections, in complete acceptance, without judgement.

And this hasn't always been the case. In the past, I gravitated toward unhealthy relationships with people who said they loved me, twisted my arm behind my back, cheated and blamed me, called abuse love, fostered feelings of rejection and shame, and insisted I play small to fit in.

Continuing on your Mastering Resilience journey means being surrounded by people who truly care about you and unequivocally support your dreams and goals. Have a mentor or a trusted coach or advisor who provides guidance, motivation, emotional support, and most importantly, Role Modeling-- because they ARE or have BEEN where you're going. This is crucial in the process of mastering resilience. For example, if you want to build a successful business, get a mentor who is successful in business; if you want help achieving your goals, choose a mentor who has a track record of setting big goals and achieving them.

*   *   *

Even the person who says, "I picked myself up by my bootstraps and did this on my own" had to rely on other people to reach those bootstraps. I guarantee it. I've had mentors my entire life. When I was young, I relied on the advice and guidance of the parents of my friends. In high school, teachers took a special interest in me, just as in college and graduate school. I have always found people in my life who I look up to as role models, and I pay attention to their methods and strategies. For my entire career as a business owner and leader, I've turned to mentors who are business coaches and advisors. I believe in developing your own personal Board of Directors. Let's face it; we live in a world full of choices with unlimited amounts of information accessible at our fingertips when we're making decisions. At any given time, I can Google how to do something and there will be thousands of possible solutions-- sometimes completely contradictory solutions!

Having a greater understanding of connections and close relationships can benefit us emotionally, physically, and mentally. Connections are another key ingredient to Mastering Resilience. When we form bonds with others, this heightens our emotional awareness of our surroundings, our goals, and our behaviors. In the field of childhood trauma, it's widely accepted that the biggest predictor of success is having a stable, dependable adult who believes in you. Identify who you surround yourself with and ask yourself if these individuals truly believe in you and your potential.

Let's go back to basics. What does it mean to have a close relationship with another person? What types of interpersonal connections do we make in our lives? For the purposes of Mastering Resilience, let's focus on three kinds of connections with others:

Deep Connections: These include loving relationships in your inner circle that may be with family and/or friends, with whom you feel safe to talk to about just about anything, including your deep feelings and insecurities.

Superficial Connections: These are friends or colleagues or people you see regularly and share common interests with, including some coworkers, baristas, fellow gym members, etc., where most, if not all of the communication is superficial.

Distant Connections: This might be distant family and friends or people who share an affiliation with you that you don't see or interact with often and when you do, you might be guarded or untrusting.

Imagine these three types of connections as circles, with the first as the innermost circle, the second as a slightly larger circle encircling the first one, and the third circle as the largest around the second.

1. Draw these three circles. The smallest circle represents the people closest to you. The medium-sized circle represents friends or colleagues. The largest circle represents distant acquaintances— including distant friends or family.

2. Place the names of your connections in each of the circles.

Mindset Shift: My true friends are individuals who let me have total freedom to be myself and especially to feel. A real friend stands up for me.

Acquaintances, friends, and family members can move between and among these types of connections, depending on the circumstances. Along your healing journey, you may start to wonder about some of your relationships. It's important that the people you keep in your innermost circle are the ones who firmly believe in you. Think about who you'd call in the case of an emergency. Which names come to mind? Who would you call if you needed a ride to a doctor's appointment? You may find out that the people you once thought were your close friends are no longer in this inner circle. Instead of sharing your most intimate feelings with all your friends and family, consider who will listen to you and help you along the way while ensuring that you're stepping into the best version of yourself. You may choose to move some of these relationships to an outer circle and have a more superficial relationship with them.

We're the average of the five people we spend the most time with, according to motivational speaker Jim Rohn. And it's certainly true that we're influenced by the people with whom we spend the most time. If you fill your inner circle with people who aren't supportive of your healing journey, it may negatively affect your trajectory. That doesn't mean you need to break off relationships. As with our earlier example of putting more nutritious food on your plate, you can add people to your inner circle who believe in you--who cheer you on and champion your goals, who allow you to be genuinely yourself, who encourage you to be the best version of yourself, people who have unconditional, positive regard for you, and the others may naturally move to the outer circles.

In a 2010 meta-analytic review of 148 studies, researchers examined the extent to which social relationships influenced risk for mortality, along with aspects of social relationships that are predictive and what factors moderate the risk. Surveying data from more than 309,000 people, they found that the absence of quality, enduring relationships raised premature mortality by 50 percent. That's roughly the equivalent of smoking some fifteen cigarettes a day. To put it in more optimistic terms, close positive relationships can potentially prolong your life.

Supportive relationships have real biological consequences. According to a study conducted by researchers at the University of California San Diego, "emotionally supportive childhood environments promote healthy development of regulatory systems, including immune, metabolic, and autonomic nervous systems, as well as the hypothalamic-pituitary-adrenal (HPA) axis, with long-term consequences for adult health." Adults with social support saw reduced physiological responses to anticipated and current stressors as well (Glynn et al., 1999).

It's imperative to acknowledge the role that positive, fulfilling, and loving relationships play in our lives, both as children and as adults. Even if you didn't have close relationships as a child, you can still work to gain them in adulthood. Close relationships help us recognize, build, and strengthen our desire and ability to live resiliently.

When I learned to have compassion for my mom, I knew I still wanted to have a relationship with her, even a superficial one. I moved her to my outer family circle in my life and chose to visit less often, to have more superficial, non-triggering conversations with her. We talked about current events, the weather, the political climate, and things that were important to her. We would have fascinating conversations that lasted for hours, yet the topics remained low stakes. Any attempt to bring up in-depth conversation ended badly. I knew I wouldn't find the maternal support I'd longed for in the past, and so I sought out and received emotional support from others in my close-knit circle. Ultimately, I accepted my mother's limitations, without judgment, and recognized that she couldn't give me this type of emotional support. You may soon recognize that certain family members and friends you cherish deeply are not equipped to give the kind of love or support you desperately need—and that's okay. You get to decide who to be vulnerable with.

Mindset Shift: It's possible to find people who truly care about me.

If you haven't found anyone to put within your inner circle, that's also okay. Start by having conversations with friends who are coworkers or others who share the same interests, or you might choose to join a local community group or a book club. Get involved with a volunteering organization, like an animal shelter. Become a member of your local faith-based community or other places where you are inclined to find people with common interest as a start. There are so many ways to find your tribe of loved ones, and to do so, you begin to recognize that vulnerability is a key ingredient in this recipe.

Brené Brown has researched shame and vulnerability for many years. In *Braving the Wilderness: The Quest for True Belonging and the Courage to Stand Alone*, she writes,

> The definition of vulnerability is uncertainty, risk, and emotional exposure. But vulnerability is not weakness; it's our most accurate measure of courage. When the barrier is our belief about vulnerability, the question

becomes: "Are we willing to show up and be seen when we can't control the outcome?" When the barrier to vulnerability is about safety, the question becomes: "Are we willing to create courageous spaces so we can be fully seen?"

Brown's definition calls particular attention to vulnerability's strength. By recasting vulnerability as courage, we're more likely to open ourselves up to new connections: new collaborators, new partners, new friends, and even new (chosen) family. Vulnerability is a key to loving relationships in life.

While Brown's work on "Courage Culture" has been critiqued for non-inclusivity, her ideas about risk and emotional exposure speak indirectly to connections and close relationships described here. Though we need to give ourselves time to heal from past adversities, we don't want to completely isolate ourselves from the rest of the world. In fact, isolation is the opposite of what we need to foster resilience, even if staying home, or staying in a safe place, may seem like the best protection from those unpredictable forces in the world. Having someone else to count on in your time of need can be extremely helpful to your mental, emotional, and physical health.

Good social relationships are tied to greater psychological health and physical well-being. So, it's not surprising that social relationships also matter when it comes to resilience, in part because they help us feel less stress when we are suffering.

People who have close relationships have:

a more positive self-image;

stronger immune systems;

better cardiovascular health;

fewer alcohol, drug, and addiction problems; and

less depression and anxiety.

Researchers at the University of Michigan in a ten-year follow-up to a large-scale population study found that positive relationships predict reduced rates of depression later in life. People who have close relationships have lower risk of death due to illness (Teo et al., 2013). Research also shows that close and intimate friends support and encourage us to live meaningful lives, pursue our dreams, be ourselves, and keep going even when we want to quit. In short, close relationships help us recognize, build, and strengthen our desire and ability to live resiliently. We don't have to do life alone.

Mindset Shift: The most powerful predictor of my relationships is the dynamic I choose to build with each person in my life.

Can we be resilient without friends? Yes, but life wouldn't be nearly as rich or meaningful. As C.S. Lewis said, "Friendship has no survival value, but it gives value to survival."

Because, yes, friendship is a matter of survival. Know how important it is to build a community of those who will go the distance with you and how you can nurture and strengthen these important relationships in your life.

Imagine climbing a mountain and having people ahead of you and behind you. The people ahead have their hands out to pull you forward and support you in making it to the top. Likewise, you can extend your hand to those coming up behind you. Whether you recognize it or not, whether it's intentional or not, interdependence happens. When you're resilient, people look up to you--they wonder how you did it!

That's one of the reasons I developed my own personal Board of Directors--a group of people I count as mentors who are willing to provide expertise as well as their true opinions. They tell it to me like it is, know me, respect my true self, and understand my areas of unique brilliance and my pitfalls. Some of them require a financial investment on my part and some of them are among my circle of friends. And not a week goes by when I don't consult with someone on my personal Board. We're all on our own individual journeys, and I encourage you to invest in mentoring. Mentors help you thrive in life as you move in the direction of your BIG Why, your dreams, vision, and goals.

*   *   *

My biological father relentlessly pursued me after I found out who he was; he was told that I knew at the age of twenty-two. He sent birthday and holiday cards, and cards for no reason other than to let me know he was thinking of me. He called me all the time. He would leave long messages for me on the tape player of my now obsolete answering machine, letting me know how much he loved me and how much he wanted to be a part of my life. When we did speak, I was often unkind to him, borrowing and expressing the same hatred my mom had. He was a big rig truck driver, and his route brought him to California from time to time. He always made a point of letting me know when he was going to be local and asked if I would be willing to meet him face-to-face. When I was twenty-seven, I finally said 'yes.'

We met at Denny's in Santa Monica, a place I rarely went. I walked into Denny's and searched for him across the room. I saw his face and saw myself. I knew I was his. There was no denying the resemblance. My mom's words sunk in, and I connected the dots. She hated me because she saw his face in me every time she looked at me and she hated him for leaving.

We talked for hours during that first meeting in the vinyl booth--it barely fit our tall frames. Our knees almost touched. We had the same hazel eyes, and they met often.

"I'm so proud of you, Lorry," he said, his smile beaming from ear to ear.

I'd never heard those words from a parent and at the time I didn't know how to process them. Part of it was because I didn't know what he was to me. And yet, his words—and his belief in me—stayed in my thoughts. The healing wasn't complete during that first meeting, but it was a start.

He made it clear that he'd loved me all along. That I was wanted. He believed in me, even though he didn't know me. My mom had sent graduation announcements and had kept my paternal grandparents apprised of my activities and he knew all that had been shared over the years and he kept track.

I didn't warm up right away. He kept sending greeting cards, trying to call and to visit as often as he could. I always knew when he would be in California. He seemed to understand that he was perceived to be at the root of the major friction between me and my mom and that grieved him. He wanted desperately for me and my mom to get along. He reconnected with my mother, and they briefly reconciled. He attended my wedding seven years after that first meeting at Denny's--as my mom's date. Though their rekindled relationship didn't last long, it was long enough for healing the hurts of their history. Their healing prompted deeper healing for me, and I experienced an even greater level of compassion for my mother.

A few years later, we were scheduled to have lunch at the Denny's near my house. I was four months pregnant with my first child. He was so excited that he was about to be a grandfather. I was his only child, and this would be his first grandchild. On this road trip in his bright blue eighteen-wheeler, he pulled into a truck stop and died of a massive heart attack.

It wasn't until after he passed away that I realized that he loved me unconditionally. No matter what I threw at him, no matter how angry I was or what I said to him, he loved me and made sure I knew it. If he were alive today, he would be in my inner circle. His persistence in loving me is something I'm grateful for. My brief relationship with him made me a better human and more devoted to those I love.

Having a greater understanding of connections and close relationships can benefit us emotionally, physically, and mentally. Connection is another key ingredient to mastering resilience. When we form bonds with others, our emotional awareness of our surroundings, our goals, and our behaviors heightens. And when you choose to build these strong foundational relationships, you will have created your own delectable cake to Master Resilience in your life.

Conclusion

*The most dangerous stories we make up are the
narratives that diminish our inherent worthiness. We
must reclaim the truth about our lovability, divinity,
and creativity.*

—*Brené Brown*

No matter what your childhood adversities were, you are a
bright spirit in this world who deserves to heal from trauma.
You've now learned the importance of having a BIG Why and
how to establish your Why NOW as you commit yourself to your
healing journey. You've learned how and why to have clarity of
your true self, as well as how to shift your thinking into actionable
steps by using the AAAs of resilience: be Aware, Acknowledge
your true self and intrinsic value, and take Action in the direction of your dreams and goals. You've learned to have compassion for yourself and others simultaneously, and you understand
how compassion plays a role in your healing journey. Finally, **you
understand that this is your time to have a Bold Opportunity
to Heal** (BOTH Approach); to consider what your future holds
and how to stay on course; and how to Master Resilience by form-
ing authentic close relationships and connections in your life.

Consider this book your recipe for your purpose. These are ingredients you can return to, whether you're baking the same cake, a different cake, or transforming those ingredients into an entirely new dish. In other words, these practices and mindset shifts can be used in your work, in your family life, in your classroom, in your practice, and, of course, in your own continued healing.

Though you're on your way to Mastering Resilience, the next step is to pay attention to how you're treating not only yourself but also the next generation and those around you. While adding these ingredients to your life, you may start to notice that old behaviors come up. Don't worry. You will always have the tools to bounce back on your healing journey, as well as the clarity about who you are uniquely (not to mention how to be the best version of yourself). Continue to hone and develop your BIG Why—your Point A and Point B—and understand that you have the ability to utilize these powerful tools to become and live as your highest self. Memorize these ingredients you've learned. Blend them into your world. You'll become a Master of Resilience in your own life. If I can do it, so can you!

Acknowledgments

Those who have been told, "You pulled yourself up by your bootstraps" rarely, if ever, do it alone. In my case, I have so many people who paved the way, helped and supported my journey. My heart is so full of gratitude.

Firstly, the author is grateful to use a collection of people over the years who represent Alex and Emma throughout this manuscript.

I would also like to thank the following:

The researchers of the original Adverse Childhood Experiences (ACE) Study, Drs. Vincent J Felitti and Robert F Anda, et.al., that made the profound connection between exposure to ACEs and how they affect physical health, mental health, social health, and economic health later in life. Dr. Nadine Burke Harris, Pediatrician, the original Surgeon General of California, who in her 2014 TEDMED Talk named ACEs as a public health crisis that requires a movement to solve. And to Bruce D Perry, M.D., Ph.D. and Oprah Winfrey, whose recent book, *What Happened to You* made the topic of ACEs understandable in a conversational way. These experts and cycle breakers, as well as many others, informed my work as a child psychologist and cycle breaker myself.

Fabienne Fredrickson, my business and mindset coach for the past ten years. Thank you for your unwavering love and support all these years in Boldheart. You were the first to tell me to write a book because my story needs to be told to help others heal and create their own impact on the world. I've learned through your example how simple (not necessarily easy) it can be to turn past adversity into your life's work.

Sara Connell, my book and thought leader coach, as well as my cheerleader, who provided the structure and accountability to get this book written and whose Voxer gifs brought joy and excitement throughout the writing process.

My developmental editor, JoAnna Novak, whose powerful nature, direct approach, keen eye, and editing expertise made my words and story come to life in order to make this book more impactful.

My fellow healers, Suzanne Longstreet, Caitlin McCoskey, and McKenzie Buzard. I am in awe of your respective gifts that you use to empower others who have lived through adversity to become the best versions of themselves and to break cycles one after the other. Your techniques have been an inspiration to me and the others who know you and work with you.

The many Accountability Buddies (ABs) over the years who held my feet to the fire and offered regular, often daily, opportunities for growth both professionally and personally, by holding me accountable to do what I said I was going to do. You know who you are. Gratitude especially to the most recent ABs, Melinda Heyford-Elston and Amanda Hinman, whose regular Voxer messages, Zoom, and phone calls held space for my lowest of lows and highest of highs during this book-writing process as well as the process of achieving the goals I set for myself during this past year. And to Ale B, the "essenceographer", who worked her magic to bring out the best of me while writing this book, and capturing it in film. From the bottom of my heart, thank you all.

Most of all, to my husband of thirty years, Gary, who relentlessly loves me and who knows the entirety of who I am. Our deep love for each other is tangible and palpable and a gift from God. And to our two adult children, Tess and Rae, who are miracles in and of themselves, who are wanted, and cherished in a profound way. They are catalysts for my ongoing healing journey, and the absolute motivation to break the cycle in this generation. I love you to the "multi-universe" and back.

Resources for Help

This book and the exercises therein are not a substitute for professional psychological services. If you, or someone close to you, needs mental health support, help is available.

To find a therapist in your area you can consult your provider directory if you have insurance, ask for referrals from your doctor and/or people you trust, look into local resources such as 211, or available online resources such as: https://www.findapsychologist.org/. Be persistent until you find the right match for you.

If you or a loved one is contemplating hurting themselves, please call the National Suicide Prevention Lifeline at 988, or visit https://www.nami.org/help.

To learn more about ACEs and find out your Number Story, visit https://numberstory.org/.

Mastering Resilience™ Resources

The Recipe for Mastering Resilience™

Before you dive into this book, I recommend that you download the free Recipe for Mastering Resilience™. This simple step by step process will act as a roadmap to help you get the desired results you are looking for in this book. I call it a recipe because there are specific ingredients, combined in a precise order, that will get you the outcome you want.

How far along are you on the Mastering Resilience Journey? Take this assessment to find out... In order to reach a new destination, we need to know our current location. In this quick assessment you'll find out where you are in relationship with each of the 8 mastering resilience ingredients. You'll learn your current score and after doing the exercises in the book, you can take the assessment again and celebrate your progress. Take the assessment now to start moving closer to your purpose immediately.

This 8-week transformational course teaches you step-by-step how to turn your past adversity into your purpose. Each week, a new ingredient is introduced, that provides specific content with guiding principles and mindset shifts that will take you through your journey of mastering resilience. You'll hear stories of real life applications and be guided to integrate the content which will transform your thoughts, feelings and behaviors. Check out the course registration and details HERE:

Super Resilient™ Youth

For those of you who are ready to get started right away with breaking the cycle in the next generation, there is the opportunity to positively impact the young people in your care. The Super Resilient™ Youth program, based on the recipe for mastering resilience, is a research-based mental wellness curriculum designed to empower youth to gain a deeper understanding of themselves to combat inner and external negativities in ways that build life-long resilience.

Additional ACEs Resources

https://numberstory.org/ Describes and offers resources to understand the story of your number and the story of your ACEs history.

 PACEs Connection is a social network that supports communities to accelerate the global PACEs science movement, to recognize the impact of positive & adverse childhood experiences (PACEs) in shaping adult behavior and health, and to promote trauma-informed and resilience-building practices and policies in all communities and institutions — from schools to prisons to hospitals and churches — to help heal and to develop resilience instead of traumatizing already traumatized people.

More Resources

As you continue applying the recipe for mastering resilience, these wonderful coaches, experts and resources may support you on your healing journey.

 Amanda Hinman is a Integrative Nutrition Health Coach and an Applied Functional Medicine Health Coach. She specializes in hormonal health.

 Suzanne Longstreet is a Mental Fitness Coach and NLP Master Coach

 Caitlin McCoskey is a body code practitioner at *A Living Well Life*. A living Well Life is a guide to wellness information and resources to help you balance and optimize your life, so that you have the ability to live your most powerful and empowered life.

McKenzie Buzard is a Rapid Transformation Therapist. Rapid Transformation Therapy (RTT) is a type of hypnotherapy created by renowned therapist, Marisa Peer.

If you are ready to make an investment in sharing your purpose with the world through a business, a book, or a lifestyle, these resources may be for you.

Fabienne Fredrickson

If you are ready to invest in support that will help you embrace your magnificence, check out Fabienne Fredrickson, author of *Embrace Your Magnificence: Get Out of Your Own Way and Live a Richer, Fuller, More Abundant Life*, and founder of Fabienne.com and the Delicious Life podcast.

Sara Connell

If you're ready to become a best selling author and speaker in less than a year, check out Sara Connell Coaching to find out how she can help you bring your message to the world.

Bibliography

ACE Resource Network. (n.d.). *Why Should I Care about My Number Story?* Your Number Story. Retrieved October 15, 2022, from https://numberstory.org/why-should-i-care-about-my-number-story/

Anderson KN, Swedo EA, Trinh E, et al. "Adverse Childhood Experiences During the COVID-19 Pandemic and Associations with Poor Mental Health and Suicidal Behaviors among High School Students" — Adolescent Behaviors and Experiences Survey, United States, January–June 2021. MMWR Morb Mortal Wkly Rep 2022;71:1301–1305. DOI: http://dx.doi.org/10.15585/mmwr.mm7141a2

Assaraf, J. (n.d.). *My Story: TURNING MY MESS... INTO MY MASTERY.* John Assaraf. Retrieved June 1, 2022, from https://www.johnassaraf.com/

Belhumeur, LL. (n.d.). *Mastering Resilience™* https://www.masteringresilience.com

Bloom, S. L. (1994). "The Sanctuary Model: Developing Generic Inpatient Programs for the Treatment of Psychological Trauma." *Handbook of Post-Traumatic Therapy, A Practical Guide to Intervention, Treatment, and Research.*

M. B. Williams and J. F. Sommer, Greenwood Publishing: 474-491.

Brown, Brené. (2017). *Braving the Wilderness: The Quest for True Belonging and the Courage to Stand Alone.* Random House.

Centers for Disease Control and Prevention. (2022, April 6). *Fast Facts: Preventing Adverse Childhood Experiences |violence prevention|injury Center|CDC.* Centers for Disease Control and Prevention. Retrieved April 1, 2022, from https://www.cdc.gov/violenceprevention/ aces/fastfact.html#:~:text=How%20big%20is%20the%20 problem,potentially%20reduce%20many%20health%20 conditions.

Cookston, J. T., Olide, A., Parke, R. D., Fabricius, W. V., Saenz, D. S., & Braver, S. L. (2014). "He said What? Guided Cognitive Reframing about the Co-resident Father/ Stepfather-Adolescent Relationship." *Journal of Research on Adolescence, 25*(2), 263–278. https://doi.org/10.1111/ jora.12120

Daly, M. (2022). "Prevalence of Depression among Adolescents in the U.S. from 2009 to 2019: Analysis of Trends by Sex, Race/ethnicity, and Income." *Journal of Adolescent Health, 70*(3), 496–499. https://doi.org/10.1016/j. jadohealth.2021.08.026

Dweck, C.S. (2006). *Mindset: The New Psychology of Success.* Random House.

Epstein, R. (1999, May 1). "Helping Athletes Go for the Gold." *Psychology Today.* Retrieved October 15, 2021, from https://www.psychologytoday.com/us/articles/199905/helping-athletes-go-the-gold

Felitti, V. J., Anda, R. F., Nordenberg, D., Williamson, D. F., Spitz, A. M., Edwards, V., Koss, M. P., & Marks, J. S. (1998). "Relationship of Childhood Abuse and Household Dysfunction to Many of the Leading Causes of Death in Adults." *American Journal of Preventive Medicine, 14*(4), 245–258. https://doi.org/10.1016/s0749-3797(98)00017-8

The Four Tendencies Quiz - gretchenrubin.com. (n.d.). Retrieved June 15, 2022, from https://gretchenrubin.com/wp-content/uploads/2022/10/Upholder-Report.pdf

Fuligni, A. J., & Galván, A. (2022). "Young People Need Experiences that Boost their Mental Health." *Nature, 610*(7931), 253–256. https://doi.org/10.1038/d41586-022-03172-y

Glynn, L.; Christenfeld, N.; & Gerin, W. (1999). "Gender, Social Support, and Cardiovascular Responses to Stress." *Psychosomatic Medicine*: March/April 1999 - Volume 61 - Issue 2 - p 234-242

Gordon, B.R., McDowell, C.P., Lyons, M. *et al.* "Resistance Exercise Training for Anxiety and Worry Symptoms among Young Adults: A Randomized Controlled Trial." *Sci Rep* **10**, 17548 (2020). https://doi.org/10.1038/s41598-020-74608-6

Grinspoon, P. (2022, May 4). "How to Recognize and Tame Your Cognitive Distortions." *Harvard Health*. Retrieved October 15, 2022.

Groth, A. (2012, July 24). "You're the Average of the Five People You Spend the Most Time With." *Business Insider*. Retrieved

May 15, 2022, from https://www.businessinsider.com/jim-rohn-youre-the-average-of-the-five-people-you-spend-the-most-time-with-2012-7

Gregory, A. A. (2022, February 20). "Why Forgiveness Isn't Required in Trauma Recovery." *Psychology Today*. Retrieved June 13, 2022, from https://www.psychologytoday.com/us/blog/simplifying-complex-trauma/202202/why-forgiveness-isn-t-required-in-trauma-recovery

Harris, N. B. (2014). "How Childhood Trauma Affects Health across a Lifetime" [Video]. TEDMED. https://www.ted.com/talks/nadine_burke_harris_how_childhood_trauma_affects_health_across_a_lifetime?language=en

Holt-Lunstad, J., Smith, T. B., & Layton, J. B. (2010). "Social Relationships and Mortality Risk: A Meta-analytic Review." *PLoS Medicine*, *7*(7). https://doi.org/10.1371/journal.pmed.1000316

Kross, Ethan. (2021). *Chatter: The Voice in Our Head, Why It Matters, and How to Harness It*. New York: Crown.

Latham, G. P., & Locke, E. A. (1991). "Self-regulation through Goal Setting." *Organizational Behavior and Human Decision Processes*, *50*(2), 212–247.

Martin Lardén, Lennart Melin, Ulrika Holst & Niklas Långström (2006) "Moral Judgement, Cognitive Distortions and Empathy in Incarcerated Delinquent and Community Control Adolescents." *Psychology, Crime & Law*, 12:5, 453-462, DOI: 10.1080/10683160500036855

Milne, S., Orbell, S., & Sheeran, P. (2002). "Combining Motivational and Volitional Interventions to Promote

Exercise Participation: Protection Motivation Theory and Implementation Intentions." *British Journal of Health Psychology*, *7*(2), 163–184. https://doi.org/10.1348/135910702169420

Op den Kelder, R., Van den Akker, A. L., Geurts, H. M., Lindauer, R. J., & Overbeek, G. (2018). "Executive Functions in Trauma-Exposed Youth: A Meta-analysis." *European Journal of Psychotraumatology*, *9*(1), 1450595. https://doi.org/10.1080/20008198.2018.1450595

Perry, Bruce D. and Winfrey, Oprah. (2021). *What Happened to You?: Conversations on Trauma, Resilience, and Healing.* Flatiron Books.

Pritchard, R. D., Roth, P. L., Jones, S. D., Galgay, P. J., & Watson, M. D. (1988). "Designing a Goal-Setting System to Enhance Performance: A Practical Guide." *Organizational Dynamics*, *17*(1), 69–78. https://doi.org/10.1016/0090-2616(88)90031-9

Priyanka, & Rasania, S. K. (2021). A Cross-Sectional Study of Mental Wellbeing with Practice of Yoga and Meditation during COVID-19 Pandemic." *Journal of Family Medicine and Primary Care*, *10*(4), 1576–1581. https://doi.org/10.4103/jfmpc.jfmpc_2367_20

Ranganathan, V. K., Siemionow, V., Liu, J. Z., Sahgal, V., & Yue, G. H. (2004). "From Mental Power to Muscle Power—Gaining Strength by Using the Mind." *Neuropsychologia*, *42*(7), 944–956. https://doi.org/10.1016/j.neuropsychologia.2003.11.018

Rubin, Gretchen. (2017). *The Four Tendencies: The Indispensable Personality Profiles that Reveal How to Make Your Life Better (and Other People's Lives Better, Too).* Harmony.

Samji, H., Wu, J., Ladak, A., Vossen, C., Stewart, E., Dove, N., Long, D., & Snell, G. (2021). "Review: Mental Health Impacts of the COVID-19 Pandemic on Children and Youth – A Systematic Review." *Child and Adolescent Mental Health*, *27*(2), 173–189. https://doi.org/10.1111/camh.12501

Schacter, D. L., Addis, D. R., Hassabis, D., Martin, V. C., Spreng, R. N., & Szpunar, K. K. (2012). "The Future of Memory: Remembering, Imagining, and the Brain." *Neuron*, *76*(4), 677–694. https://doi.org/10.1016/j.neuron.2012.11.001

Sharma, A., Madaan, V., & Petty, F. D. (2006). "Exercise for Mental Health." *The Primary Care Companion to The Journal of Clinical Psychiatry*, *08*(02), 106. https://doi.org/10.4088/pcc.v08n0208a

Sohn, E. (2022, August 24). "Tackling the Mental-Health Crisis in Young People." *Nature News*. Retrieved October 15, 2022, from https://www.nature.com/articles/d41586-022-02206-9

Teo, A. R., Choi, H. J., & Valenstein, M. (2013). "Social Relationships and Depression: Ten-year Follow-up from a Nationally Representative Study." *PLoS ONE*, *8*(4). https://doi.org/10.1371/journal.pone.0062396

Toxic Stress. Center on the Developing Child at Harvard University. (2020, August 17). Retrieved April 15, 2022, from https://developingchild.harvard.edu/science/key-concepts/toxic-stress/

Tseng, J., & Poppenk, J. (2020). "Brain Meta-State Transitions Demarcate Thoughts across Task Contexts Exposing the Mental Noise of Trait Neuroticism." *Nature*

Communications, 11(1). https://doi.org/10.1038/s41467-020-17255-9

Vigna, A.J., Poehlmann-Tynan, J. & Koenig, B.W. "Is Self-Compassion Protective among Sexual- and Gender-Minority Adolescents across Racial Groups?". *Mindfulness* 11, 800–815 (2020). https://doi.org/10.1007/s12671-019-01294-5

Whitlock, J., Mai, T., Call, M., & Van Epps, J. (2021, February 4). "How to Practice Self-Compassion for Resilience and Well-Being." Retrieved October 13, 2021, from https://accelerate.uofuhealth.utah.edu/resilience/how-to-practice-self-compassion-for-resilience-and-well-being

Yazeed, C. (2021, December 12). "The Dangers of Courage Culture and Why Brené Brown Isn't for Black Folk." Dr Carey Yazeed. Retrieved October 15, 2022, from https://drcareyyazeed.com/the-dangers-of-courage-culture-and-why-brene-brown-isnt-for-black-folk/

Zimmerman, M. J., & Bradley, B. (2019, January 9). "Intrinsic vs. Extrinsic Value." *Stanford Encyclopedia of Philosophy.* Retrieved February 3, 2022, from https://plato.stanford.edu/entries/value-intrinsic-extrinsic/

About the Author

Lorry Leigh Belhumeur, Ph.D. is an Educator, Child Psychologist and Leader of leaders, influencers and allies of youth. Her life's mission is to transform trauma into one's purpose and positive impact in the world. She is passionate about breaking the cycle of the negative impact of Adverse Childhood Experiences (ACEs) and toxic stress caused by persistent exposure to ACEs and other types of adversity. She is especially committed to preventing the serious impact of ACEs and adversity on the mental health and well-being of children and those who care for them. She is the author of the *Transformational Course, Mastering Resilience*™: *Living on Purpose*, that promotes taking action consistent with one's purpose, through learning and applying her recipe for mastering resilience. She is the co-author and presenter of "Using Data to Reverse the Impacts of Adverse Childhood Experiences." She has written and spoken on the topics such as "Resiliency: Your Mental Health Matters," and "Understanding ACEs: Teaching and Practicing Resilience," both locally and internationally.

CPSIA information can be obtained
at www.ICGtesting.com
Printed in the USA
BVHW041935100423
662076BV00001B/31